CONTENTS

9 Courting A Legend

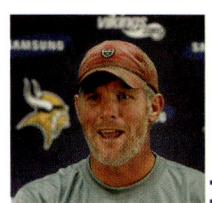

17 Favre Arrives

35 2009 Preseason

47 2009 Regular Season

109 Photo Gallery

FOREWORD

What is the hardest thing to do in sports? Here's a clue: It's not hitting a curveball in a blizzard during an outdoor World Series game at Target Field, or sinking a 60-foot uphill putt on the final hole of the PGA Championship as Tiger Woods stares laser beams that seep into your practice swing. It's not being Manny Ramirez' hairdresser or the solitary sad safety that stands in the way of Adrian Peterson as he explodes to the goal line.

Here's the hardest thing to do in sports: Live up to the hype. Brett Favre has done it for almost 20 years, and what he's accomplished so far in his first season in Minnesota is astounding. His persona has a solar system all its own, with the national media hanging on his every word, innuendo and text message. He was expected to do wonderful things for the Vikings, but that wasn't enough. He's turned so many moments into magic already. While the road so far has already been thrilling, the final script of the 2009 season has yet to be written. As it plays out on fields from Minneapolis to possibly Miami, enjoy this look back at what one of the most fun and exciting seasons Minnesota football fans have seen in years. As he always does, Brett Favre is living up to the hype. And then some!

Tom Zenner

Editor in Chief

Sport Publishing

Everything you've heard about Brett Favre is true.

True, Favre is the quarterback the Vikings needed to make them a complete team.

True, Favre makes the other players better, and they were already some of the best personnel in the NFL.

True, Favre makes the Vikings among the favorites to play in the Super Bowl.

True, Favre's success and the Vikings' dominance of the NFC North has led to record television ratings and made the Vikings one of the most publicized teams in the NFL.

Yes, it's all true. It's also true that the leadership the 40-year-old quarterback provides is as important as his play, and experts are saying he hasn't lost a thing on the football field. The confidence he gives his teammates might be as important as the final-second, winning touchdown pass he threw to beat the San Francisco 49ers, as significant as the great performances he provides in most every game.

There was concern about the chemistry in the locker room with the addition of Favre and the demotion of other quarterbacks who had been with the team.

But I've covered this team from Day 1 of its existence, and Mr. Favre has created a positive situation in the locker room, one that has never been better.

And he is so happy here that I wouldn't bet two cents that if he leads the Vikings to a Super Bowl victory he won't come back to try for a second ring.

Sid Hartman

Star Tribune Columnist

Purple Reign!

BRETT FAVRE'S INCREDIBLE JOURNEY TO MINNESOTA— AND THE MAGICAL RIDE HE'S LED VIKINGS' FANS ON IN 2009

StarTribune

Sport Publishing

President: Jim Pouba
Editor-in-Chief: Tom Zenner
Chief Designer: Marlon Cantillano
VP Sales & Marketing: Don Kapral
Editor Assistant: Brooke Dashavana
Web Designer: Will Bradley
Design Consultant: Tony Kardell
Research: Lawson McKenzie
For special orders: www.startribunepurpleqb.com

StarTribune

Editorial Team

Editor, Senior Vice President: Nancy Barnes
Assistant Managing Editor, Sports: Glen Crevier
Assistant Sports Editor: Chris Miller
Senior photo Editor: Deborah Pastner
Sports Photo Director: Tricia Drury
Reporters: Mark Craig, Chip Scoggins, Judd Zulgad
Jim Souhan, Patrick Reusse, Sid Hartman

Photographers: Elizabeth Flores, Jim Gehrz, Judy Griesdieck, Carlos Gonzalez, Kyndell Harkness, Jerry Holt, David Joles, Renée Jones Schneider, Brian Peterson, Richard Sennott, Jeffrey Thompson, Richard Tsong-Taatarii, Tom Wallace, Jeff Wheeler

Business Team

Senior Vice President, Advertising: David Walsh
Vice President, Classified Advertising/Niche Products: Jamie Flaws
Director of Niche Products: Christina Savin
Project Manager: Lori Sebastian
Web site: www.startribune.com
and www.accessvikings.com

ISBN: 978-0-615-33732-6

All rights reserved. Except for use in a review, the reproduction or utilization of this work in any form or by any electronic, mechanical, or other means, now known or hereafter invented, including xerography, photocopying, and recording, and in any information storage and retrieval system, is forbidden without written permission.

This book is available in quantity at special discounts for your group or organization.

For further information, contact the publisher.

Printed in the United States

Sports Publishing, LLC
www.Sport-Publishing.com
sales@sport-publishing.com
Tel/fax: (708) 401-0076

Courting a Legend!

Courting A Legend

Favre is a perfect fit for Vikings offense

Mark Craig, *StarTribune*

The Vikings would be insane not to sign Brett Favre if they believe his right arm will be healthy enough to play this season.

They have room under the salary cap and nobody who's better at quarterback, and Favre wants to be here. And, oh yeah, it wouldn't cost them a draft pick or a player.

Other than ESPN annexing Winter Park, where's the downside?

In 2007, the New York Jets were 4-12 without Favre. In 2008, with a healthy Favre completing 71 percent of his passes through the first 11 games, the Jets doubled their victory total to 8-3 by upsetting the undefeated Titans in Tennessee.

A healthy Favre threw 20 touchdown passes in 11 games and made the Jets a much better team. An ailing Favre threw nine interceptions and caused them them go 1-4 down the stretch.

So it seems like an easy call at Winter Park. If the medical staff believes Favre's torn right biceps is easily repairable or will heal soon, Favre joins the Vikings and they become a better team.

If his arm goes kablooey, the Vikings simply return to Plan A, Sage Rosenfels and/or Tarvaris Jackson. If Favre stinks it up after eight to 10 games, there's no John Madden Rule that says the Vikings can't bench or release him altogether. Plenty of Hall of Famers have been released before. Jerry Rice, the greatest receiver in NFL history, was cut when he couldn't make it as a fourth receiver in Denver.

From a purely football IQ perspective, signing a healthy Favre is a no-brainer. He'd be in a West Coast offense that's similar to what he ran in Green Bay. He also would be paired with a great running game and a solid defense, both of which should lessen Favre's desire to take risks with the football.

Yes, Favre throws interceptions. But here's a stat for you: In the 29 games before his arm and shoulder began hurting last season, Favre threw 23 more touchdown passes than interceptions (53-30) and led the Packers to an NFC title game.

One of those touchdown passes perfectly illustrates the savvy playmaking ability a healthy Favre offers that Jackson and Rosenfels don't at this time. It came Sept. 30, 2007, at the Metrodome.

The Packers were facing third-and-7 at the Vikings 16-yard line. Receiver Greg Jennings was split wide right. Tight end Donald Lee was tight right.

The call from the sideline was a pass to the left side. But Favre saw an opening across from Jennings on the right.

With the play clock ticking down, Favre didn't panic. He used a hand signal to let Jennings know he was switching the play to "Dragon."

That told Jennings he'd have to switch his route to a slant pattern. But there was a problem. Lee hadn't seen the hand signal and was about to run a pattern that would have collided with the slant being run by Jennings.

Favre simply ran over to Lee, yelled "Dragon" into the left ear hole of his helmet, ran back and got the ball snapped with the play clock at :01.

Jennings ran the slant pattern. The first window

of opportunity to throw the ball closed quickly. Favre waited. Jennings kept slanting toward the goal line.

The second window opened and, as Madden would say, "Bam!" Favre threw it. Jennings caught it. And Dan Marino's career record for touchdown passes fell with Favre's 421st TD.

"It was a perfect read by Brett," Jennings said that day. "But that's what we expect from him. He sees everything on the field."

For this to work in Minnesota, Favre would have to spend time at Winter Park during the offseason. He would need to be there when there's actual football being taught, because his new set of receivers would need to learn ASAP how his mind works on game day in this offense.

Then, perhaps someday, when it's third-and-7 in the red zone and the play clock is almost expired, one of those purple-clad receivers will know to switch his route, sprint past the first window and look for one of those Favre bullets coming through that second window.

Of course, that's only if the Vikings truly believe that 39-year-old gun can be back up and slinging in less than four months.

Courting A Legend

May 9, 2009

Favre's dance choreographed with precision
His waffling in the media is driven by a desire to dodge spring OTAs; his itch to play on is fueled by a weird insecurity

Patrick Reusse, StarTribune

There were a few hours at mid-afternoon Friday when Brett Favre seemed ready to be in the background of national sports coverage. ESPN was ready to puts its focus on Alex Rodriguez's return to the Yankees lineup and the Dodgers' second game with Manny Ramirez missing.

Favre and his agent, Bus Cook, could not put up with this. Perhaps Chris Mortensen and Ed Werder were bored with the pair, because they found a new bobo within the ESPN empire to leak information: Jeremy Schaap.

He came up with the report at 2:45 p.m. that Favre had sent X-rays of his right shoulder to the Vikings. Apparently, this shipment was taking place Thursday, at the same time Yahoo! Sports felt it had scooped the world with a revelation that Favre told Vikings coach Brad Childress not to bother meeting him in Mississippi -- that this time, the quarterback truly was retired.

And, we might as well throw this one out while we're at it: A rumor has circulated locally that the Vikings sent an orthopedic specialist to Mississippi this week to check out Favre.

What would seem to be going on here with Favre is the same delicate balancing act he has attempted to pull off for the past several years.

The contention here is that the conflict with Favre never has been between playing and retiring. The conflict has involved continuing to play and figuring out how to avoid the organized team activities (OTAs) that now take place for a total of four weeks before and after minicamp.

The spring practices have been around for a while, but organizations recently applied the OTA label and put more pressure on players to attend.

The first time the term was used with the Vikings was in 2006, with Childress as the coach. That was also Mike McCarthy's first season in Green Bay. And it was also the first time Favre chose to start the offseason with a mention of possible retirement.

Two years later, Favre turned the 2008 offseason into a daily drama: sobbing over retirement, vacillating on a return, getting angry when the Packers decided to get on with their lives, and winding up unhappy with the New York Jets.

Clearly, he enjoyed the attention, since he has decided to create the same chaos in 2009. Remember when this all started -- the ESPN report that included the information the Vikings would expect Favre to fully participate in the team's offseason program?

That had to give Packers GM Ted Thompson and McCarthy a chuckle -- the idea their division rivals were naive enough to think they could get Favre to spend most of five weeks at Winter Park for a minicamp and OTAs.

Even if Favre signs, this is what we're going to hear: The old boy needs some rehabilitation on his shoulder, he can do that as well in Mississippi as in Minnesota, and the Vikings expect that he will be throwing in time for several OTA days in mid-June.

I haven't been around Favre enough to attempt psychoanalysis. So, a Wisconsin reporter was asked to put the quarterback on a couch.

Question: The theory that this return is motivated by a hatred for the Packers' Thompson. Is it valid?

Reporter: "I buy the revenge factor, although I don't buy that it's as deep with Brett as with his

Purple Reign!

family. His wife (Deanna) has got it bad when it comes to loathing Thompson. His family as a whole wants Brett to play to get back at the Packers. Plus, they enjoy watching him."

Question: This would seem to validate that he both suffers and is driven by an over-the-top sensitivity to criticism -- a Kevin Garnett in a helmet?

Reporter: "A shrink who wanted to win a Nobel Prize would do an extensive study on Brett and where he comes from. There's this remarkable dichotomy between a brilliant athlete with supreme confidence on the field, and a guy with enough insecurities to never miss a game, even when he probably should have, and who tried to keep his backup from taking more than a few practice snaps.

"He got his job because Don Majkowski missed a game with injury. In my opinion, that on those days he's with his football team, he never forgets that."

Courting A Legend

May 13, 2009

Burning bridges between Favre fans

Most Packers fans gathering in Hudson, Wis., still cherish their former QB, but that could change if he ever dons purple

Patrick Reusse, *StarTribune*

HUDSON, WIS. - There are signs placed around Lakefront Park intended to prevent behavior that some people might find offensive: No Smoking, No Feeding Ducks or Geese, and No Loitering (an odd restriction for a park).

The city fathers have not yet ordered signs reading: No Wearing Favre Jerseys. Presumably, these will be erected should it come to pass that Brett Favre, Green Bay's famous No. 4, signs with the cross-river Vikings in the hours before the start of training camp.

On Tuesday, a Packers promotional tour made a stop at Lakefront Park's bandstand. A program was scheduled to start at 6 p.m., featuring team president Mark Murphy and players Nick Collins, Brady Poppinga and Jordy Nelson.

The parking spots within several blocks of the park were occupied a couple of hours early. Members of the organizing committee were found near an entrance.

"This is the first time the Packers brought their tour to Hudson," one organizer said. "We had 650 tickets for the autograph party, and they sold out the first day. We'll have more than 1,000 people, compared to about 300 people that they had last night in Marshfield."

Patrick Johnson, 16, from Hudson was placing a framed Favre jersey in the back of his family's truck. The garment was autographed and under glass.

"Are you selling now that Brett's going to wind up with the Vikings?" Johnson was asked. The young man shook his head and said: "I just want people to be able to see it. I'm not selling."

The group parked next to the Johnsons had a large Favre cutout. They had placed a paper bag over Brett's face. A visitor said: "You thought he was a god for 15 years, and now he's covered with a paper bag?"

Denise Boron said: "He's still a god. No matter what happens, the years in Green Bay are what everyone will remember about Brett."

Tom Boron, her husband, said Packers fans are comfortable with the idea that they will have a better quarterback this season in Aaron Rodgers than will the Vikings, even with Favre.

"The Vikings could've had Rodgers, and instead they drafted (Erasmus) James, the defensive end from Wisconsin," Tom said. "Do you think they would like to do that over?"

Last season, the Vikings opened the regular season on a Monday night at Lambeau Field. Rodgers made his first start.

A Minnesota reporter walked through several blocks of tailgaters. The most popular jerseys were Favre's No. 4 for the Packers. And there were more Favre/Jets jerseys than Rodgers' No. 12.

That has changed. On Tuesday night, Rodgers' 12s were more in evidence than Favre's 4s. Dillon Rutten, 11, was among those honoring the current Packers quarterback.

Tim Rutten, his father and a Packers' season-ticket holder, said: "Dillon's not a front-runner. He got this jersey before the start of last year."

The older Rutten said he will remain a Favre admirer, even if he were to sign with the Vikings. He admits that could put him in a minority with the team's zealots.

PURPLE REIGN!

"If he ends up with the Vikings, there are going to be a lot of hard feelings in Packerland," he said. "Most of the Jets games were on television in Wisconsin last year. I don't think there will be demand for Vikings games on TV because of Favre."

Doug Martinek, a Packers fan from North St. Paul, was wearing a Rodgers jersey. He works in Mendota Heights and has been hearing a daily stream of "Favre in purple" conversation from his co-workers.

"It's their (Vikings fans) time to get on us," Martinek said. "All I can say is, `We got the best out of him.' "I hear some Packers fans say, `I'll always be a Favre fan, even if he signs with the Vikings.' That's baloney.

"If he goes with the Vikings, he will have thrown away his legacy as a Packer. I've been done with him since last year, when he said he wanted to play for the Vikings.

"I saw some quotes this week from (former Packer) LeRoy Butler that I agree with 100 percent. LeRoy said that Brett going to the Jets was sticking it to (Packers GM) Ted Thompson, but going to the Vikings ... that will be sticking it to the fans."

FAVRE ARRIVES

Favre Arrives

August 19, 2009

Brett Favre, Minnesota Viking

Chip Scoggins, *StarTribune*

For years it was inconceivable, as improbable as Magic Johnson joining the Celtics or Larry Bird the Lakers. Last year we all rubbed our eyes and couldn't believe it was a possibility, but Brett was a Jet instead. This summer's shocker was that this thing felt like a done deal, but we were fooled again by the story that wouldn't die. Or so we thought. Like the maniac in a horror movie, this story just cannot be killed. Today, it's not only alive, it's finally, undeniably, unbelievably true. Brett Favre, Minnesota Viking.

Brett Favre was on his way to throw passes to a high school team near his home in Hattiesburg, Miss., on Monday afternoon when his cell phone rang.

On the other end was Vikings coach Brad Childress, who wanted to check one final time to make sure the future Hall of Fame quarterback was sticking with his decision to remain retired.

Three weeks after telling Childress no thanks, Favre gave him a different answer this time. "When Brad called, it was kind of like, `This is it. Now or never,'" Favre said.

That conversation ended a long, strange soap opera -- jokingly dubbed "Favre-a-palooza" by one Vikings player -- that ultimately ended with a surreal scene outside Winter Park on Tuesday as the 39-year-old Favre arrived to a hero's welcome before donning a purple helmet for his first practice.

Vilified by Vikings fans for years as he built his legend in Green Bay, Favre was mobbed by several hundred fans as he pulled into the team's facility in an SUV driven by Childress.

Favre agreed to a two-year, $25 million deal, including $12 million guaranteed this season, and then took part in a two-hour practice. Afterward, Favre said he postponed retirement a second time because he didn't want to live with any regrets.

"I just didn't want to look back," he said. "I have no idea how I'll feel a year from now, five years from now, 10 years from now. But I didn't want to have to say `what if.'"

Favre's health remained the biggest hurdle throughout the process. He underwent surgery to fix the torn biceps tendon in his right arm in May, but he revealed Tuesday that he learned around the same time that he also has a tear in his rotator cuff.

Dr. James Andrews told Favre the rotator cuff injury was not new because there is some calcification around the tear. Favre admitted the news "scared" him because he didn't want to go through another situation like last season when he struggled down the stretch with the New York Jets while dealing with arm problems. Favre received assurance from Andrews that he could play with the rotator cuff injury without needing more surgery.

Even so, the Vikings publicly had closed the door on Favre three weeks ago, before the start of training camp, when he told Childress that he would stay retired. But it didn't take long before Favre began having second thoughts. "Believe me, at times I felt like, `I hope I didn't make the wrong decision,'" he said. "But I knew I had to deal with it."

That all changed with Childress' phone call. Childress described his 11th-hour pursuit as a "small window" to pull off a "unique opportunity." This time, Favre jumped at the opportunity, even asking Childress whether he can play in Friday's preseason game against the Kansas City Chiefs at the Metrodome.

"Everyone who I've talked to -- former players, coaches, people in general -- said if you were to go back, this is a perfect fit," Favre said. "Once again, there's no guarantees, but they have a really good football team here, a very good running game, and

Favre Arrives

I hope from my standpoint, I felt like all along that I could offer some experience and leadership.

"I have to admit, through this whole process after I said `no' three weeks ago, at times I was OK with it. Other times I said, `Boy, you know, I feel like I could help that team.' I think that's the competitive fire in me. As a player, regardless of sport, you have to feel like you can make a difference. And I truly feel like I can."

Favre admitted it felt "different" putting on a purple helmet after spending 16 seasons with the rival Packers. He reiterated that he isn't concerned about whether Packers fans feel betrayed by his decision.

"The bottom line is that it's football," he said. "Once people start chasing you and once you step into the huddle, I don't look at the helmets, I look at the faces. I think the guys will know I'm in it for the right reasons. That's because I still love to play. Regardless of who it's with, I still feel like I can help this team or whichever team was willing to take a chance.

"I know there are people out there taking sides or whatever. This is not about revenge, believe me. You can't take away the 16 years I had in Green Bay; it was unbelievable and it was great. That will be forever cherished by me and the guys I played with. They've moved on and I've moved on, so I think it's great for football."

But what about his legacy? Favre's waffling ways has become the source of both jokes and frustration. His response? "Don't watch," he said. "First of all, when people start talking about my legacy, it's mine," he said. "It's what I think of it. I know the way I play the game. I know the way I handled myself as a teammate, as a leader, within the public. Yeah, I've made mistakes along the way, we all have. But if I had to do it all over again, I would do it the same way.

"I don't think anyone has played the game with as much passion and has loved it and loved his teammates as much as me. I haven't always been the best player. I would like to think that every player that I have played with would love to have me in the foxhole. I have no idea what is going to happen this year. I didn't know last year. As I look back, I gave it everything I could give. That's what I'll do this year."

NUMBERS

9:10 a.m. -- Favre boarded a plane for the Twin Cities, touching off a day's worth of breaking news reports locally and nationally.

2 and 25 -- Years and millions of dollars for Favre's contract. This year: $12 million. Next year: $13 million.

Favre Arrives — August 19, 2009

Dazed and confused
For Packers fans, Tuesday's news was a punch to the gut: Their hero for 16 years has traded green and gold for purple.
Patrick Reusse, StarTribune

Jim Bougie is the bar manager at Gabe's Roadhouse, the St. Paul eatery and saloon that gets taken over by a Packers horde whenever the lads from Green Bay are in competition.

"We had 150 of them in here on Saturday night," Bougie said. "(Aaron) Rodgers looked good. They all left happy." Bougie smiled. "Not today," he said. "I just heard on the news that the St. Croix River is rising. Tears from Packers fans."

Gary Scott, a Gabe's regular, said: "They are in the parking lot here at 9 o'clock on Sunday mornings, with their jerseys and hats, waiting to get in. "Who knows? Maybe this means we're going to be able to take back our bar."

Bougie shook his head and said: "They love their team and spend money. We want Packer fans."

The bar manager smiled again and said, "Even if most of the Wisconsin people I know wake up at point-0-8 in the morning."

Tuesday was a time of giddiness for Vikings followers and of stiffening upper lips for Packers fans. Brett Favre finally signed with the Vikings -- timing his arrival to miss all offseason work, to miss training camp and to miss the opening exhibition on the road.

There's nothing Favre seeks more than adulation, and he will get all that an egomaniac can handle when his on-field unveiling as a Viking takes place Friday night in the Metrodome.

Favre's presence in Minnesota will be tied to another plea from coach Brad Childress, as well as the quarterback's familiarity with offensive coordinator Darrell Bevell.

The opinion here is the timeline offered Tuesday is a charade -- that the Vikings and Favre decided last month to reconnect in mid-August.

What shouldn't be underestimated is Favre's ability to read Zygi Wilf, and see that he was dealing with a star-struck owner willing to allow the quarterback to dictate terms.

"I'll be there in mid-August -- not a moment earlier -- and you'll pay me $12 million" was Favre's message.

To which Zygi clearly responded: "Thank you, Mr. Favre, and could we bother you for an autographed football for me and the entire Wilf family?"

Nick Gardner, 21, is a Minnesota Duluth senior from Rhinelander, Wis. "I really thought -- after what he said three weeks ago -- that this time he was done," he said. "This is a terrible day for Packers fans.

"And those that are saying, `I've moved on; I don't care about Favre anymore,' you know what? They are trying to convince themselves.

"You can't have a player who quarterbacks your team for 16 years -- who means everything to the Packers and football in Wisconsin -- and say it doesn't mean anything that he now will be playing for the big rival. "We're all dying inside."

It will get worse for Gardner in four days when he arrives back in Duluth. "I'm badly outnumbered on campus," he said. "I'm not looking forward to Oct. 5 (Vikings-Packers in the Dome). The week before that game is going to be brutal."

Roberta Gherty works at a coffee shop and also a pizza place in downtown Hudson, Wis. She's known to locals as "Bert." Her car is painted in

Packers colors.

"I saw some Vikings fans getting excited and cheering Brett," Gherty said. "We're in shock over that, but we're going to come out of it."

As Hudson's ultimate Packers loyalist, Bert was asked if there were any tears as Favre arrived in Minnesota as if he was Napoleon returning to Paris -- and, by coincidence, both conquering heroes in ridiculous hats.

"No tears; I shed those when he left the Packers," Gherty said. "I thought I was over Brett completely. I even went out and bought a Rodgers jersey. "I don't know what I'm going to do with my collection of Favre jerseys now that he's with the Vikings. Maybe I'll put them all up for sale."

K.P. Anderson, formerly of Cambridge, is the executive producer of E! Television's "The Soup" and the spinoff "Sports Soup" on Versus. He heard the Favre news when he awoke in L.A. on Tuesday morning and turned on television.

"First thing I did was call the writers and say, `Tiger Woods choking isn't a top story anymore.' We're going with Favre and more Favre.

"The video of people waiting along the road for Favre ... I don't recall my fellow Vikings fans doing that when we got Sage Rosenfels."

Favre Arrives — August 19, 2009

Wilf pleased with finally landing Favre
The Vikings owner got to know the quarterback on a private flight from Mississippi, affirming his opinion.
Sid Hartman, StarTribune

Zygi Wilf, owner of the Vikings, said he was as shocked as anybody else would have been when he got a phone call Monday from coach Brad Childress saying that he had made a phone call to Brett Favre and the former Packers quarterback had changed his mind about retiring to join the Vikings.

"I had our plane ready to fly to Minnesota (from New Jersey) Tuesday morning, planned to watch practice on Tuesday and then fly to Chicago for a league meeting on Wednesday," Wilf said. "It all happened in 24 hours. Instead of flying to Minneapolis we went to Hattiesburg (Mississippi) to pick up Favre, and if he passed a physical, he was going to be a Viking."

Terms had been set long before the last conversation with Favre. Wilf had insisted that Favre not get a guaranteed multiyear contract as part of the negotiations.

So the way things worked out, Favre will get a two-year contract. The first year of $12 million will all be guaranteed once the season starts. The second year calls for Favre to be paid $13 million, but none of it will be guaranteed.

Wilf insisted the signing wasn't to sell tickets but basically to improve the team.

Wilf, his son, Jonathan, and his brother Mark were on the private plane flying back here from Mississippi. Word that Favre was heading north spread quickly. At one point during the flight, an air-traffic controller in Memphis asked the pilot if he might have an old quarterback on board.

Wilf said he was very impressed with Favre during the two-hour flight. "Very much so. He's a guy who can bring confidence to everybody on our ballclub," Wilf said. "You know from his actions and the way he talks he has a love for the game. He's committed to winning.

He'll give his all to do the best he can." What impressed you the most about him? "He's such a regular top guy. It was a pleasure just to hear from him," Wilf said. "He has a love and passion for the game. That's all you can ask. To be coming from a future Hall of Famer like Brett Favre is special to see. He is ready to go.

"This is something the fans have been looking forward to for a long time. Like I have always stated: Our personnel department and our team will do everything necessary to make our team better. We have done that from year one."

Do your people feel he has a lot of football left in him? "Absolutely. His love of the game and desire to play and knowing that, from his standpoint, he wouldn't be doing this unless he knows he can do this," Wilf said.

How did it finally happen?

"It just happened. The timing was right," Wilf said. "We both felt good that he could come aboard. It was the desire and the love to play football. It was an opportunity to play football and have a club that wanted him to play for them us."

Do you think he can take you to the Super Bowl?

"All I can say is that it makes us a better team," Wilf said. "Any time we get better, our chances get better to do what we set out to do, and this year it's defend our division (title) and move on. We are very optimistic about our chances this season of improving."

Does this help the stadium deal?

PURPLE REIGN!

Favre Arrives

"We didn't approach it from that aspect," Wilf said "There is an urgency right now to get the Vikings stadium deal done. I am sure with the cooperation of the Legislature and all the people in Minnesota, we will find a way to get it done.

"It will certainly help us sell tickets. But the most important objective was to get our team to be a better team. I think today we just got a little bit better."

Big day for Bevell

Darrell Bevell had worked as Favre's quarterback coach for three years in Green Bay before becoming Vikings offensive coordinator.

"I am excited about him for our football team," Bevell said. "He has a proven track record. He is a great talent. I look forward to having him on our offense."

Bevell was asked if there any one thing he recalled about coaching Favre. "I remember him not missing a start. He played every game whether he was hurt or not. Obviously, I remember his talent," said Bevell, himself a former quarterback.

Do you remember any certain game or play he made?

"One of my fondest memories is the Monday night game when we went down to Oakland the day after his father passed away," Bevell said.

"He played out of his mind and played outstanding."

Do you think he has lost much?

"That remains to be seen. I don't think he has lost much," Bevell said. "He has only been in here for one day. We need to give him a little bit of time before we answer that fully."

When you went down to Hattiesburg and saw him work out did you believe he could still play?

"It was an opportunity to look at him physically, in terms of how the ball was coming out and was he able to release it without pain," Bevell said. "He was honest with us, and told us for the most part there wasn't much pain. He threw close to 100 balls that day, and still looked good."

Did seeing him one day bring back memories?

"It's fun to watch him. He is great for the game," Bevell said. "To see Favre on the back of the jersey is going to be exciting for our fans."

How does he fit in with this offense?

There is definitely a place for him," Bevell said. "We need a leader. He knows the offense, and knows where to go with the football. We know exactly what kind of performance we are going to get when we send him out there."

How are guys going to profit from him?

"A lot of guys are going to profit from him. A lot of guys are going to benefit from him," Bevell said.

"He's a good player. He's definitely one of the best who has ever played the game. We need to get that out of him while he's here." Vikings fans might have dreamed of Favre playing for the team, but what were the odds that would happen?

And can you imagine the scene in Green Bay when the Vikings play the Packers in that Monday night game on Oct. 5?

If Favre is healthy and can perform anywhere near how he did two years ago when he led the Packers to a 13-3 record and one pass interception from going to the Super Bowl, the Vikings with the great defense and now a great quarterback could be in Miami when they play the Super Bowl next February.

Favre Arrives

Mariucci has faith in Favre's ability
The former Green Bay assistant coach watched his former pupil practice, and liked what he saw

Sid Hartman, *StarTribune*

Brett Favre walked off at the end of practice Wednesday and the first thing he did on the sidelines was approach Steve Mariucci, an old friend who coached the new Vikings quarterback for four years while they were with the Green Bay Packers.

The conversation between Mariucci, who had watched Favre for the whole practice, and the quarterback continued for more than 30 minutes. Mariucci later said he came away with the opinion that the future Hall of Famer still can play with the best.

"I was there when he was a baby, his first four years (in Green Bay). I am watching him throw today in practice, and he looks to me like he's making all the same kind of throws," said Mariucci, the former 49ers and Lions head coach who is now with the NFL Network.

"It looks like his arm is sharp, fresh and healthy," said Mariucci, an outstanding football coach, first in college at California and then with the pros. "I don't know if he's feeling any pain or not, but he looks sharp. It's interesting to be able to jump right off the bus and jump right in the huddle and run this offense. It's all familiar to him."

So he looks as good as ever?

"Let's watch him throw in pads. Right now in shorts he looks good to me. It's a good start," Mariucci said.

So you think he can be the difference in how the Vikings do?

"Oh, yes. At a lot of levels, not just his throwing," said Mariucci. "His knowledge and experience in the system. His leadership. If it comes down to the last drive and you need it, people in the huddle will believe he can do it. He's been there so many times. He brings a lot of experience."

Mariucci believes fans will follow Favre's progress nationwide.

"It's going to be a lot of fun. I think a lot of football fans around the country, whether you are a Packer fan or Viking fan, will be interested to watch the (soon-to-be) 40-year-old play," Mariucci said.

Any advice for him?

"Have fun. He doesn't have any trouble doing that," he said. "He loves playing football. Everybody knows that. He loves the game, he loves to compete."

Why do you think he came back?

"Because of what I just said: He can't get enough," Mariucci said. "He feels like he can play, and has an opportunity to play here. He seems to be healthy.

What other advice did you give him?

"I just said let it rip, and have fun," said Mariucci. "He's not going to start second-guessing any decision. He has made a commitment to this organization, and is going to go for it. I think we all know that with him, they have a pretty good chance to do some damage in this NFL chase."

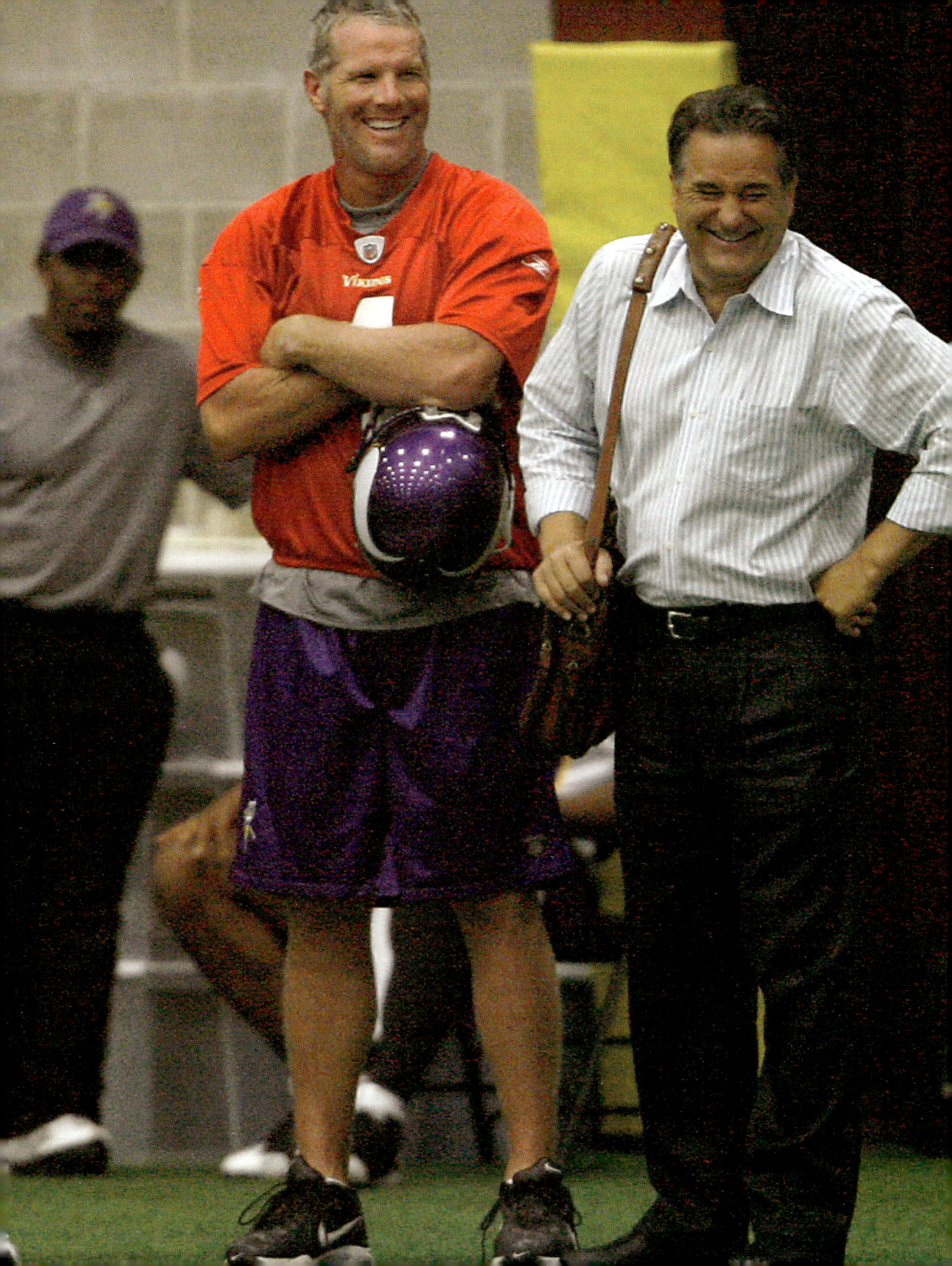

2009 Regular Season
September 13, 2009

Childress confident all pieces are in place
The Vikings open a new season after three years of steady improvement, and the coach sees great potential

Sid Hartman, *StarTribune*

As the Vikings prepare today to face the Browns in Brad Childress' fourth season opener, the head coach believes the team has "gotten better and better."

"The biggest thing you look at is, obviously, to see if you can improve talent and continuity," Childress said. "We've been able -- the Wilfs (team owners) have allowed us to keep all this coaching staff together. I think the draft picks (this year) are guys that will contribute. We did it with a particular eye towards special teams -- with the safeties we kept, with the backup linebackers we kept -- so I think that will help. And, obviously, adding a quarterback, I think, makes us better." Naturally, the big move was adding veteran quarterback Brett Favre.

"I think he made a quick jump from week one to week two, from four days of practice to one week of practice," said Childress. "I think that will continue to evolve, because we'll be talking about growing even at the end of the season, whether it's growing with his relationship with the tight ends, or (receivers) Bernard Berrian or Sidney Rice or with the running backs. I think that will just continue to evolve."

Childress said the chemistry is good on the team despite media reports to the contrary. Favre's arrival might have been especially upsetting to quarterbacks Sage Rosenfels and Tarvaris Jackson, but that's not the case.

"(Favre has) kind of endeared himself to them as well," Childress said. "Those guys have a good room and good exchange. They have fun in there with Kevin (Rogers, the quarterback coach). (Favre is) all about wanting to win. He doesn't need the money right now, he doesn't need the commercials. He wants to win and he wants to win with the Vikings."

Another newcomer, receiver Percy Harvin, has gotten as big a buildup as any recent top draft choice, including running back Adrian Peterson.

"He missed that first (preseason) game and this last one, but I think he's as advertised in terms of having the quicks and being able to contribute in the return game," Childress said. "We'll get him involved here as we go. It remains to be seen how many times we can put his hands on the ball. There's only one ball, though, for Berrian, Peterson, Harvin, (tight end Visanthe) Shiancoe and Favre."

Yes, the Vikings record under Childress has improved as good players have been added. Former coach Bud Grant, who had great success with the Vikings, will tell you that the coaching role is exaggerated. The team with the best players wins.

I believe Childress has done a great job during his three past seasons here. He has put together a good coaching staff. In my visits with general managers and coaches around the NFL, they have sung the praises of Childress, who proved himself worthy of the accolades by winning the division last year.

Packers colors.

"I saw some Vikings fans getting excited and cheering Brett," Gherty said. "We're in shock over that, but we're going to come out of it."

As Hudson's ultimate Packers loyalist, Bert was asked if there were any tears as Favre arrived in Minnesota as if he was Napoleon returning to Paris -- and, by coincidence, both conquering heroes in ridiculous hats.

"No tears; I shed those when he left the

Packers," Gherty said. "I thought I was over Brett completely. I even went out and bought a Rodgers jersey. "I don't know what I'm going to do with my collection of Favre jerseys now that he's with the Vikings. Maybe I'll put them all up for sale."

K.P. Anderson, formerly of Cambridge, is the executive producer of E! Television's "The Soup" and the spinoff "Sports Soup" on Versus. He heard the Favre news when he awoke in L.A. on Tuesday morning and turned on television.

"First thing I did was call the writers and say, 'Tiger Woods choking isn't a top story anymore.' We're going with Favre and more Favre."

"The video of people waiting along the road for Favre ... I don't recall my fellow Vikings fans doing that when we got Sage Rosenfels."

2009 Preseason

2009 Preseason
August 22, 2009

Favre did not look right in purple

Jim Souhan, *StarTribune*

Brett Favre jogged onto the Metrodome turf Friday night wearing purple, looking as odd as Prince in plaid.

The Vikings jersey looked wrong on him, as if it had been photo-shopped. "'It was surreal, seeing him in that," said receiver Bobby Wade. "It was an awesome experience, though."

Favre's debut wasn't. He took seven official snaps in two series, throwing three incompletions, and wedging a short pass in to Percy Harvin.

He received a standing ovation, then went 1-for-4, completing one more pass than each of the people in the stands wearing their brand-new No. 4 jerseys. One guy wore a purple T-shirt and taped "Favre 4" onto the back. "It's a lot different than in the past," Favre said. "I was honored. I am honored."

After his cameo, Favre retired to the sideline. Well, maybe in his case we should choose a different verb. This being one of those meaningless, overpriced, boring preseason games, Favre's performance proved ceremonial and anticlimactic.

Apparently when he was practicing with Oak Grove High he didn't have to face a blitz. Favre looked rusty and uncomfortable, and took a big hit to the chest on his last pass attempt.

Did he want to play more? "After that last hit," he said, "I thought I'd wait until next week."

What Favre brings even during a brief and unproductive performance in an unsightly preseason game is presence.

The Vikings have employed plenty of competent, promising, or accomplished quarterbacks in the last couple of decades.

Daunte Culpepper put together one of the all-time great seasons for an NFL quarterback in 2004. Randall Cunningham reached the NFC title game. Rich Gannon and Brad Johnson apprenticed here on their way to a Super Bowl meeting. Jim McMahon and Warren Moon stopped by.

That's a pretty good list, but none of them, even at their best, commanded the attention Favre does. Even with a convicted dog-fighter joining one of the league's most successful franchises, Favre is the No. 1 story in the NFL, and he has made the Vikings the league's most intriguing team.

Favre also brings certainty to the position for the first time since, oh, 2004, when Culpepper was at his best.

Whatever his faults, Favre gives the Vikings an unquestioned starter, a veteran who won't prompt speculation about his imminent replacement if he has a bad quarter, half or game.

Before the game, there were fans wearing No. 4 jerseys ringing the stadium, waiting for Favre to appear. Inside the Dome, when he jogged onto the field fashionably late --at 6:21 for a 7 p.m. game -- the cheering began.

If you were hoping for something more than the typical boring, meaningless preseason game, you probably were disappointed. Mostly, we spent the night allowing our eyes to adjust to the jarring sight of No. 4 jogging out of the Vikings' tunnel wearing purple.

After the game, Favre stood at the customary starting quarterback locker, wearing a T-shirt and a Vikings cap, drawing double-takes from just about everybody.

"'Yeah, it is weird," tight end Visanthe Shiancoe said. "'You have Brett Favre in purple. Think about it. Brett Favre in purple.

"'He's taller than I thought, too."

Tackle Bryant McKinnie glanced at Favre and said, "'I'm not going to lie, it's strange. For eight years, he was the enemy, and now he's right over there."

Favre admitted to being nervous before the game. Late Friday night, he admitted he was happy he didn't fumble a snap or call the wrong play. ``Getting this game over is probably a good thing,'' he said. ``I know we'll be judged later, down the road.''

Three days after coming out of retirement, he also said: ``I know I made the right decision.''

2009 Preseason   **Vikings 17/Chiefs 13**   August 22, 2009

Call it a glorified glance
Brett Favre was a less-than-fabulous 1-for-4 in two series, but he was warmly received at his new home stadium.
Judd Zulgad, *StarTribune*

As Brett Favre sat in his hotel room Friday waiting to play his first game with the Vikings, he experienced a feeling he hadn't had in a long time.

A 19-year veteran, three-time NFL MVP and two-time Super Bowl participant, Favre realized he was nervous -- for a preseason game. "All of a sudden I started having butterflies," Favre said. "That was probably the oddest thing. I was talking to my oldest daughter and she was telling me good luck and all this stuff. I said, `I'm nervous.' She said, `Oh, you'll be fine.' I just don't want to screw up."

Favre spoke after playing two series in the Vikings' 17-13 victory over the Kansas City Chiefs before an announced crowd of 67,782. Three days after deciding to end his retirement, the 39-year-old completed one of four passes for 4 yards. But he did not "screw up" by fumbling a snap or throwing an interception.

The performance might not have earned Favre any style points -- Tarvaris Jackson, on the other hand, completed 12 of 15 passes with two touchdowns, no interceptions and a perfect 158.3 passer rating -- but it did help him begin to shake off some of the rust that had built up since he announced in February that he was calling it quits again after one season with the New York Jets.

With the Vikings not playing again until a week from Monday in Houston, coach Brad Childress won't have his team practice again until Tuesday. That will give Favre a bit of time to catch his breath. His whirlwind week has included plenty of excitement, including starting a game in the Metrodome, a building in which he was reviled during his 16 seasons with the Green Bay Packers.

"It felt a little odd, so many years being on the other side," Favre said. "But I thought it was a welcome reception. I know in the long run, we'll be judged on wins and losses. I'm well aware of that. This is a tough place to play. It's nice to be on the other side. It was a little loud when we were on offense, too. But I think this place is just loud, period."

Favre's brief appearance was a prelude to what likely will be a much longer stint in in Houston. His biggest adjustment is going to be getting back in game shape and getting on the same page with other members of the offense. His familiarity with the terminology in the West Coast system will be a plus.

"I don't think there was anything really that conceptually he had to think too much about," Childress said. "We really didn't game-plan so you just have a play list that is functional, where you can see people play. ... Snap count, hard count; he got one of our guys on a hard count. That's something that you have to build, too."

Favre was in for seven plays. He took the field with 12 minutes, 6 seconds left in the first quarter after Vikings linebacker E.J. Henderson recovered a fumble that ended the opening drive of the game.

Favre received a standing ovation as he trotted onto the field to join the huddle after taking some extra time to talk things over with offensive coordinator Darrell Bevell. Favre missed on three of his four passes. His completion came when rookie wide receiver Percy Harvin made a nice diving reception. Favre also took two hits from linebackers, including a solid shot by a blitzing Corey Mays as Favre threw an incomplete pass.

"He's going to get hit, it's football," Childress said. "But he's put together well and takes good care of himself."

Favre said his nerves were brought on by far

more than putting on a purple jersey for the first time after so many years of wearing the Packers' green and gold. In fact, Favre said donning a New York Jets jersey a year ago helped make the fact he wasn't wearing Packers colors seem not so odd. So what was wrong?

"That's a good question," he said. "Maybe (having) 2 1/2 days of practice. Live bullets, no red jersey and of course all the attention that has been focused on this. ... With all that attention it's hard not to feel like you have to live up to all this hype. Not that I don't want to do that. The most important thing is to lead this team to victory.

"I didn't want to get off on the wrong foot. I wanted to call the plays right, get in and out of the huddle, be as smooth as possible. Based on the fact there were 2 1/2 days (of practice) I consider that a small victory tonight."

DAZZLING? NAH, BUT STILL A MEMORABLE DEBUT

Friday night's preseason game against Kansas City marked Brett Favre's first appearance with the Vikings. Here's how the evening went:

- Favre came out for pregame warmups sat 6:20 p.m. as a sparse crowd documented the moment with cell-phone photos.

- On the Vikings' first possession, Favre joined the offense on the field during a TV timeout as hundreds of flashbulbs popped from the nearly filled Metrodome stands.

First play: Favre handed to Adrian Peterson for a 4-yard gain.

First pass: Favre threw incomplete to Fahu Tahi on second-and-6 from the Vikings 48.

First completion: Favre hit Percy Harvin for 5 yards on third-and-6 on the next play.

First wipeout: Favre was buried by Corey Mays on his second series and threw incomplete, finishing his night 1-for-4.

- On the Vikings' third series, Tarvaris Jackson took over at quarterback and was greeted by boos. But Jackson threw a pair of touchdown passes to put the Vikings into a second-half lead.

2009 Preseason — **Vikings 17/Houston 10** — September 1, 2009

Two good for the long haul
Adrian Peterson scored on a 75-yard run on the first play, and Brett Favre looked healthy and effective.

Judd Zulgad, *StarTribune*

HOUSTON - There was little doubt who the marquee attraction was Monday night at Reliant Stadium.

Two weeks after joining the Vikings, Brett Favre played into the third quarter of his team's 17-10 victory over the Houston Texans.

The future Hall of Fame quarterback threw his first touchdown pass as a member of the franchise, twice lined as a wide receiver as the Vikings unveiled their version of the Wildcat offense and even threw a vicious block from that formation.

And if that wasn't enough, Favre also caused a pregame stir when ESPN reported he might be playing with a cracked rib. But no matter what Favre was able to accomplish in his first extensive action in purple, one thing was made abundantly clear to the Vikings and a national television audience.

This remains Adrian Peterson's offense.

Playing in his home state, the running back rushed for 117 yards on 11 carries with a touchdown. That score came on the game's first play from scrimmage, when Peterson took a Favre handoff and went 75 yards.

"Those guys did a great job up front," Peterson said of his linemen. "You have to give all the credit to those guys. I was untouched."

Said Vikings coach Brad Childress: "You can't start much better than that. It punches a hole in things."

Peterson's heroics likely reaffirmed to Favre why the Vikings were such a good fit for him. Favre looked shaky in his first action with the Vikings, playing two series (1-for-4) against Kansas City only three days after joining the team. He appeared far more comfortable Monday before being replaced by Tarvaris Jackson.

Favre completed 13 of 18 passes for 142 yards with a touchdown, no interceptions and a 113.7 passer rating. "I think he is getting more comfortable with this offense," said tight end Visanthe Shiancoe, who had two catches for 30 yards. "There is a lot of promise here. We still have a lot of work to do, but from what we have seen as an offense, Brett has done pretty well."

Favre's TD pass came while directing the two-minute offense in the second quarter and was capped with a short toss in the flat to Chester Taylor that the running back took 28 yards for a score. Favre, working from the shotgun, avoided a corner blitz to get the pass off.

"I'm not going to make a big deal one way or the other about last week or tonight," Favre said. "I think I got better tonight as opposed to last week. I know I'm up against the clock. We start playing next week for real. Overall, I'm pleased. I felt like I took another step forward more so than anything, getting familiar with the guys.

"But you can also see how we've had some penalties and things that fall back on me. ... So there are some things I'm not pleased with. I feel good about what's in front of us. I think that we can be very productive but we've got to get it together pretty quickly."

Penalties continued to be an issue for the Vikings. After being assessed 23 penalties in the first two games, the Vikings were called for 13 on Monday and nine were against the offense. This included five on Favre's last drive in the third quarter when the Vikings were called for an illegal formation, an illegal substitution, two false starts and the crackback block by Favre. Favre threw the low block on Houston safety Eugene Wilson, who

left the game because of a knee injury.

That block was especially surprising considering Favre, who will turn 40 on Oct. 10, has a torn rotator cuff in his throwing arm, had surgery on the same arm in May to repair a biceps tendon and now is bothered by sore ribs after taking a hit to the midsection from Chiefs linebacker Corey Mays on Aug. 21.

ESPN reported that in a production meeting with Favre over the weekend, he indicated he might have a cracked rib. Favre said after the game that while the hit hurt, he doesn't believe the rib is cracked. "I haven't had an X-ray yet but even if it shows there's a crack, there is nothing you can do about it, just play with it," he said.

Childress, for one, appeared fairly satisfied with Favre's play.

"I thought he did some good things in terms of putting the ball where it needed to be," Childress said. "He'd be the first to tell you he probably missed a couple of reads and made a couple of plays with his feet. Had enough pocket presence to be able to move around and still complete the football. So obviously a big improvement."

2009 Preseason — Vikings 17/Houston 10 — September 1, 2009

After his final drive, Favre starts to look a little less lost
At the end of the first half, he began to show glimpses of what Brad Childress was looking for in the quarterback.

Jim Souhan, *StarTribune*

HOUSTON - Before the Vikings faced Houston, we learned Brett Favre had revealed to ESPN that he might have a cracked rib. ESPN's Adam Schefter immediately reported that Favre was suffering from a "rib schism."

During the game, the Vikings had Percy Harvin take the snap with Favre splitting wide left. Schefter noted that no Vikings went left with him, and broke the news that the Vikings will term this their "Schism Formation."

Being named Favre means every utterance and rumor regarding him will lead "SportsCenter." Being named Favre also provides insulation from criticism as he learns the Vikings offense, because every misstep can be excused as part of his acclimation.

Until late in the first half Monday night, Favre needed the insulation more than an ice fishing house on Lake Minnetonka in February. At that point, Tarvaris Jackson and Sage Rosenfels had performed better than Favre had this preseason.

Just when you were tempted to hand him a walker and a bowl of bran, though, the tenderized old quarterback who skipped training camp began to tease as only he can.

Not until the Vikings took the ball on the 27 with 3 minutes, 38 seconds remaining in the first half did Favre hint he might be worth the gas Brad Childress burned picking him up from the airport two weeks ago.

"Before that, we were saying, `Let's not go out like this,'" tight end Visanthe Shiancoe said. "You could see him get a lot more comfortable, though. He was on a roll. The whole offense was on a roll. He's a vet, and he showed why we brought him here."

Early in that drive, Favre threw an awful, wobbling pass deep down the right sideline to Jaymar Johnson, and he was lucky it wasn't intercepted. At that point, Favre was 5-for-9 for 42 yards. He had looked indecisive on a few throws and afraid to get hit on a few others.

Then Favre delved into the archives to produce the kind of drive that used to haunt Viking fans. He completed his last six passes of the first half -- although two were wiped out by penalties. Facing third-and-3 from the Texans 28 with 37 seconds remaining in the half, he spotted a corner blitz and quickly dumped a pass to Chester Taylor, who needed to break only one tackle to score.

Favre ran down the field celebrating -- somewhere, John Madden was saying, "Brett Favre just loves football" -- and we had our first indication since he stopped throwing to Oak Grove High players that he could make a difference this season.

"Being here 12, 13 days, and having that type of test, I thought it was a good thing," Favre said.

The touchdown didn't require a difficult throw, just the right throw at the right time following the kind of split-second decision that often wins or loses games in the NFL.

Of course, if Jackson or Rosenfels had thrown that pass, Taylor would have received all the credit.

Favre looked lost in his first game, and he looked a little less lost but just as unproductive in his second -- until that last drive of the first half.

Starting with that drive, and counting completions wiped out by penalties, Favre completed 12 consecutive short passes. He finished 13-of-18 for 142 yards and no interceptions.

He even threw an illegal block on his last drive

-- an illegal crackback out of the Wildcat formation that injured a veteran safety (Eugene Wilson) in a preseason game.

It was a cheap play. Favre said he didn't intend to hurt Wilson, but felt he had to block for his teammate.

Whether you believe Favre has cracked ribs or shouldn't have thrown the cheap crackback block; whether you believe he's rounding into shape or ready for assisted living, let's face it: He's Brett Favre, and he has seized our undivided attention.

2009 Preseason — **Dallas 35/Vikings 31** — September 5, 2009

Backup plan still murky

Sage Rosenfels and John David Booty struggled, and the QB the team wants to trade, Tarvaris Jackson played little.

Judd Zulgad, *StarTribune*

Brad Childress knows he has his starting quarterback now that Brett Favre is wearing purple. But with eight days until the regular-season opener in Cleveland, the Vikings coach cleary isn't happy with his quarterback situation as a whole.

That became clear after Sage Rosenfels and John David Booty threw third-quarter interceptions that were returned for touchdowns in the Vikings' 35-31 loss to Dallas on Friday night in their preseason finale before an announced crowd of 62,334 at the Metrodome.

"At times (the quarterback play) was embarrassing," said an upset Childress, who rarely is critical of his players in his postgame news conferences. "I'll end up putting that on myself. Not having them ready to come out of the locker room at halftime. But all the quarterbacks I've ever coached have some regard for the football, and you can't throw it to them."

Friday's game was supposed to serve as a platform for reserves, including the quarterbacks, to step forward and give the Vikings coaching staff and executives something to think about today as they cut the roster by 22 players to the regular-season limit of 53 by 5 p.m. Starters did not play Friday, and many of them, including Favre, stood on the sideline wearing sweatpants and T-shirts.

While Rosenfels and Booty gave Childress plenty to think about, much of it wasn't positive. In fact, Tarvaris Jackson was the only quarterback who had a solid performance, and he was the guy the Vikings were shopping to other teams this week as they debated whether they should carry four quarterbacks on the active roster.

Jackson started and played through the Vikings' first series of the second quarter, completing two of four passes for 42 yards with a touchdown and a 127.1 passer rating. Rosenfels entered in the second quarter and finished 7-for-15 for 115 yards with a subpar 45.1 rating; Booty was worse, going 7-for-13 for 85 yards with a 42.1 rating. Childress said he benched both quarterbacks after their interceptions, meaning Booty replaced Rosenfels, threw one pass and then was lifted for Rosenfels.

"It always seems like you want to take back one play, and I wish I could take that one back," Rosenfels said of a pass that was picked off by Cowboys cornerback Pat Watkins and returned 23 yards down the near sideline for a touchdown. "It was just a bad play by me. Other than that, I felt real comfortable out there, and I thought I did a pretty good job executing the offense other than that one play."

But that one play was enough to draw Childress' ire, as was Booty's miscue. That came on second-and-7 from the Vikings 39-yard line when Cowboys linebacker Steve Octavien stepped in front of a pass intended for wide receiver Vinny Perretta and went 44 yards for a touchdown.

Booty showed that he remains a long way from being ready to play on a regular basis at the NFL level. He was in for the Vikings' final drive of the game and missed badly on a second-down pass for Bobby Williams from the Dallas 26-yard line and again on fourth down on a pass for Perretta.

In fairness to all three quarterbacks, they were playing with backup players and not front-line guys. That did little to improve Childress' mood. Asked what he could have done to have gotten better results from Rosenfels and Booty in the third quarter, Childress said, "Just having them more prepared to come out and ready to rip to start the second half."

While it's possible Vikings officials already

have made their decision about the quarterback situation, the thought of trying to trade Jackson has to be a whole lot less palatable for Childress and Co. this morning. One option could be trying to get Booty through waivers and then putting him on the practice squad, something that is possible because he was active for only one game in 2008.

Childress certainly didn't give Booty a ringing endorsement late Friday night. "He has progressed," Childress said. "But short of telling you whether he is on the roster, he's not on the roster. He's in the middle of it and it's always an evolution. There are some things he is better at and some things he needs to get better at."

Childress was frustrated, but he also had to be breathing a sigh of relief as he left the Metrodome. If the Vikings had been unable to talk Favre out of retirement three weeks ago, what they witnessed Friday would have been the battle for the starting job instead of a backup battle that, while frustrating, doesn't have the potential to derail a season with high expectations.

As long as the nearly 40-year-old Favre can stay healthy.

2009 Regular Season

2009 Regular Season
September 13, 2009

"It's part of my life"

Brett Favre did not want to play out his career with another team, but he still feels as if he has what it takes to play at a high level. And, obviously, so do the Vikings.

Judd Zulgad, *StarTribune*

The once-revered quarterback was wearing an unfamiliar uniform and looking old and beat up.

Surely this wasn't how the quarterback wanted to be remembered, a teenager in the crowd thought. A player once known as a gunslinger now just holding on.

This memory stayed with the young fan into adulthood, serving as a cautionary tale. This was one mistake that wasn't going to be repeated. Not by Brett Favre, at least.

For it was Favre who was in the Louisiana Superdome that day watching Kenny Stabler -- a name synonymous with the Oakland Raiders -- finish his career with the New Orleans Saints. It was Favre who saw what can happen when great things are expected of a quarterback placed in a foreign environment. And it was Favre, entering his 14th season with the Green Bay Packers, who recounted all of this in 2005.

"I couldn't wait to see Kenny Stabler come out of the locker room," Favre told the Wisconsin State Journal, remembering the trip he took to see the Saints with family members in the early 1980s. "He came out and his hair was all long, his uniform was hanging off of him -- his better days were behind him. I just remember, to the fans, he was just the savior. Boy, once they got him in New Orleans, he was going to turn them around. Well, that didn't happen.

"I'd hate to go somewhere else and have everybody say, `Hey, we've got Brett.' I mean, too many great things have happened for me here (with the Packers). And if it ends tomorrow, it ends tomorrow. But I don't need to go somewhere else and prove anything."

It has been four years since Favre told that story. Yet, as Favre gets ready to play his first regular-season game today as a member of the (this still seems odd to write) Minnesota Vikings today in Cleveland, it seems more poignant than ever.

Less than a month from his 40th birthday, Favre can only hope he's never the subject of a similar tale.

How did we get here?

So much has happened to Favre since 2005. His head coach in Green Bay changed from Mike Sherman to Mike McCarthy. He believed Ted Thompson, the Packers general manager, forced him to make too quick a decision about his future after the Packers went 13-3 in 2007 but lost in the NFC Championship Game to the New York Giants.

Favre retired in a tearful news conference at Lambeau Field in March 2008 but changed his mind and asked to return a few months later. When the Packers told him it was too late, the sides ended up going through a bitter divorce that ended with Favre being dealt to the New York Jets. He retired again after last season, only to return to the Vikings on Aug. 18 after a summer of flirting with the Packers' archrival.

At his introductory news conference, Favre was asked about how he would respond to all of those who were tired of his inability to walk away.

"Don't watch," he shot back. "Like my old (Packers) roommate and center for a long time, Frank Winters, who is from Hoboken, N.J., and has a funny way of putting things, (said), `Dude, it's America. You know, it happens all the time.' "

What makes it so interesting is that Favre was

2009 Regular Season
September 13, 2009

so sure this wasn't going to happen to him. Maybe some other dude. Favre wasn't going to continue playing just for the sake of it. He wasn't going to put himself in the position of being someone else's savior. And, one would think, he certainly wasn't going to ever wear purple and don the horns.

But Favre overestimated his ability to walk away from the game. It's almost certainly the same thing that happened to Stabler and numerous other great athletes who looked so odd playing their latter years in another uniform (think Unitas, Montana, Aaron and Mays).

"It is tough" to retire, Favre said last week. "To say it's part of my life is an understatement. I think more than anything when you feel you can still do it ... there's a lot of guys who would love to (keep playing) but can't, either from injury or just ability. I still feel I can still play at a high enough level. ...

Two years ago, I felt I had the best year in my career. If anything, that may have reinforced to me that I still could play at a high level." They know the feeling.

His waffling already has turned many against him, but plenty know exactly what he's going through.

"It's ridiculous how hard it is (to quit)," Hall of Fame quarterback Dan Marino said. "Especially when you play at a certain level for so long and have had such success. It's something your whole mind and body is attuned to be ready to play in the fall. That first year after I retired it drove me crazy. Not playing."

Marino spent all 17 of his NFL seasons with the Dolphins, establishing numerous passing records, but he toyed with the idea of joining the Vikings or Steelers in 2000 before deciding against it, in part because he felt physically he could no longer continue. Marino, who will turn 48 on Tuesday and is now in his eighth year an NFL studio analyst for CBS, said the scary thing is that your mind might never convince you of what your body knows.

"It's funny, too, like I go to a couple of Dolphins preseason games and you get down on the field and you're around the players, and it's like you feel like you're ready to go," said Marino, who was 38 when he quit. "It almost never leaves you, you know?"

Steve Young certainly does. Another decorated quarterback, Young was NFL MVP in 1992 and 1994 while playing for the 49ers. He retired after playing only three games in 1999 and was inducted into the Pro Football Hall of Fame alongside Marino in 2005.

"It's a very difficult thing," said Young, who was forced to retire at 38 after suffering four concussions in three years and is now an analyst for ESPN. "Think about any profession, any highly skilled profession, surgeon or whatever, you are world-renowned, and at 38 or 40 they say, `You can't cut it anymore.' And you say, `But I'm great at this.' Forget about being great at anything else; you're not even good at anything else.

"That call you keep hearing, that doesn't go away. Retiring is like falling off a cliff. There's a lot of damage done, and you have to get up and recover. Brett's kind of opened the book on the difficulties of making that decision. At times it's comical, at times it's heartbreaking, and you're watching it play out right in front of you. The longer you play, the harder it gets."

The health issue

Marino's and Young's physical conditions at the time of their retirements meant they had little choice but to file their papers with the NFL. Former Vikings QB Rich Gannon, who was named the league's MVP in 2002 while playing for Oakland, also was forced to retire because of a serious injury. Yet, Gannon admits he gave thought to trying to return.

"I had broke my neck in 2004 and the following year I had a phone call from Jon Gruden down in Tampa saying, `Hey, come on, we can do this thing,' " said Gannon, an analyst for CBS. "My mind started wondering and thinking, `You

2009 Regular Season

September 13, 2009

know what? I might like to try that.' This was after breaking my neck.

"From Brett's perspective, it's completely different. Here's a guy that's healthy, that's hardly ever had any injury problems. He has been very durable."

Favre will play in his 272nd consecutive regular-season game today, putting him 11 games from breaking Jim Marshall's long-standing record for a non-kicker or punter. Favre also has made 269 consecutive starts, a streak that dates to the fourth game of the 1992 season.

Yet, Favre was bothered in the second half of last season with the Jets by a torn biceps tendon in his throwing arm that required surgery in May. He admits he's playing with a partially torn rotator cuff in his right arm and speculated he might have cracked a rib while taking a hard hit in his first preseason appearance.

Favre remains healthy enough to play, but at his age, he is certainly at risk to suffer an injury that leaves him no choice but to give it up.

"Once you stop, you can't come back," said Vikings offensive coordinator Darrell Bevell, Favre's quarterbacks coach for three seasons in Green Bay. "I think probably the guys that he talked to, all those guys told him that. Guys like Jim Kelly, John Elway, Steve Young. Once you're done, you're done. All those guys still would love to play, and I'm sure when they watch games they say, `Shoot, I could make that play right there.' I think that will always be there."

But eventually, that almost Peter Pan-like outlook has to be overcome with a decision that, while extremely difficult, is also realistic. Although that might no longer be the case, Favre certainly knew that in 2005.

"I don't see myself like a Kenny Stabler," he told the State Journal. "No offense to him, he had a great career and he was a great quarterback. But I see myself as a Packer, and that's it. I don't ever see myself in another uniform. And when it's time, I hope I know."

2009 Regular Season   Vikings 34/Cleveland 20   September 13, 2009

Much more than 4

Judd Zulgad, *StarTribune*

The Vikings trailed at halftime, until their superstar running back broke matters open with 155 rushing yards in the second half. Brett Favre played his first game for the Vikings and got a great view of Adrian Peterson taking over in a victory. Another significant newcomer, top draft pick Percy Harvin, also stood out, as a receiver and a kick returner.

CLEVELAND - The statistical line will say that Brett Favre's debut with the Vikings was nothing special. The quarterback completed 14 of 21 passes for 110 yards, with one touchdown, and was sacked four times.

But while the Vikings' 34-20 victory Sunday did not feature Favre in a starring role, it did provide an answer, or actually two, as to why the future Hall of Famer wanted to end his second attempt at retirement to play in Minnesota. Their names are Adrian Peterson and Percy Harvin, and they have the potential to make Favre, not to mention coach Brad Childress, look very good.

The pair did exactly that Sunday at Cleveland Browns Stadium, with Peterson rushing for 180 yards and three touchdowns on 25 carries. Harvin, making his NFL debut, caught three passes for 36 yards, including a touchdown, and averaged 33 yards on three kickoff returns.

"I had a blast," Favre said after making his 270th consecutive regular-season start. "It wasn't a 400-yard passing game, but it doesn't have to be. I'll be the first to tell you that. I'll take that any day of the week, as long as we win. That's what it's all about."

The Vikings' season-opening victory, their third in four years under Childress, won't earn them any style points. They did not use their version of the Wildcat offense and certainly did not appear to throw open the playbook just because Favre is running the show.

But what they did manage to do was earn an efficient victory in the type of game that some of Childress' previous teams might have struggled to win. The Browns are coming off a 4-12 finish in 2008 and, under new coach Eric Mangini, they were looking to give the home fans reason for optimism.

Cleveland managed to do that in a lethargic first half, leading 13-10 after two quarters. Joshua Cribbs' 67-yard punt return for a touchdown late in the half had the potential to send the Vikings into a spiral.

Instead, the opposite happened.

The Vikings made a halftime adjustment to address safety blitzes the Browns were sending and proceeded to outscore Cleveland 24-7 in the final two quarters. The Vikings, who went three-and-out on their final three drives of the opening half, ran 22 offensive plays in the third quarter compared to six for the Browns.

"When you haven't played extended snaps together, it takes a little bit of time to play off of each other," Childress said. "That is what first games look like. I'm happy to be able to get out of here with a win."

Peterson deserved much of the credit for the Vikings' success. He averaged only 2.8 yards on nine first-half carries and went to the locker room shortly before halftime to get intravenous fluids. Peterson returned a man possessed and rushed for 155 yards over the final 30 minutes.

This included a remarkable -- even by Peterson's standards -- 64-yard touchdown run in which he broke five tackles before racing down the far sideline. "I haven't played with a running back like that," said Favre, who is entering his 19th season. "He's pretty awesome, but I guess that's an understatement."

Said Peterson: "That is some good stuff coming

from Brett Favre. It makes me feel really good. I just continue to work hard and prepare each week to play the best I can."

Harvin, the 22nd pick in the first round of the NFL draft last April, also gave a glimpse of his ability as a playmaker. Harvin's 6-yard touchdown catch late in the third quarter came only because he stretched his 5-11 frame as far as possible after catching the ball at the 3-yard line and extended it to the goal line.

Favre's first touchdown pass as a Viking was the 465th of his career, extending an NFL record he set against the Vikings in 2007. "I don't know how many I've thrown, but they've all been a blast," Favre said when asked how meaningful his latest touchdown pass was to him. "Some maybe have had more meaning than others, but I was pretty excited. Had we scored running the ball, I'd have been equally as excited. But that one ranks up there near the top."

Harvin's most important reception of the day occurred on the same drive with the Vikings facing second-and-18 from their own 21-yard line. Favre, working out of the shotgun, found Harvin wide open, and the receiver went 21 yards to keep the Vikings alive.

"They did a tremendous job," said wide receiver Sidney Rice, who had only two receptions Sunday but drew a pass interference penalty at the Browns 4 to set up the Vikings' first touchdown of the third quarter. "Percy catching the ball, squirting into the end zone. It's a great job getting into the end zone, and Adrian, he's just going to be Adrian. You can expect that from him every week."

And that's something Favre is looking forward to, especially because it means defenses are going to have to pick their poison when facing the Vikings. "It's a risk/reward thing against us," Favre said. "If you're playing against us you're going to say, `Are they going to throw 40 times a game or hand it to Adrian 40 or whatever times? Now, how do we want to approach that?' I don't have an answer to that."

The Vikings' hope is that neither do many of their opponents.

2009 Regular Season — Vikings 27/Detroit 13
September 21, 2009

Stepping on the gas
Even Brett Favre could see a half-empty glass after somewhat uneven Vikings victory left them at 2-0

Judd Zulgad, *starTribune*

DETROIT - The Vikings left Ford Field on Sunday atop the NFC North with a 2-0 record. Both victories have come on the road, they have outscored opponents by 28 points and Brett Favre has yet to throw an interception.

So all is going according to plan in the land of Purple, right?

Not exactly.

Favre made that very clear after the Vikings rallied for a 27-13 victory over a Detroit Lions team that has lost 19 in a row, second-most in NFL history.

"To think that we can continue to win games that way, is not going to happen," Favre said. "Detroit played hard, played well. I was worried. ...

"I don't care how good you are or how good you think you are. You still have to play. We came back and scored a lot of points. Did what we needed to do finally. But we can't continue to do that. ... We've got to find a way to do it from the start."

For the second week in a row, the Vikings looked average early against a weaker opponent. In the opener, the Cleveland Browns took a 13-10 halftime lead before the Vikings stormed back with 24 unanswered points. On Sunday, the Lions held a 10-0 lead late in the second quarter before the Vikings went on a 27-0 run. Chad Greenway intercepted Lions rookie Matthew Stafford twice and also recovered a fumble to lead the Vikings defense.

Before anyone gets too excited about the Vikings' ability to rally, keep in mind the Browns and Lions were a combined 4-28 last season. Things are going to get much tougher next Sunday when the Vikings play their home opener against unbeaten San Francisco.

While Childress admitted the tempo was not where the Vikings wanted it in the first half Sunday, he also pointed out there is "no such thing as a bad win." Childress likely wasn't so kind behind closed doors, and many of his players echoed their coach's true feelings afterward.

"Not to take anything away from those guys, but it was a lot about what we were doing," said running back Adrian Peterson, who rushed for 92 yards on 15 carries and a touchdown. "Looking at the guys you say, `Hey, are y'all ready to play now?' We came out flat. If it wasn't me, it was someone else messing up offensively. You really can't be productive and create a drive like that."

Peterson's reference to his own miscue involved a first-quarter fumble he lost that killed a Vikings drive at the Lions 48. It was Peterson's first fumble of the season -- he had an NFL-high nine in 2008 -- and his fifth in the past three games against Detroit.

That fumble, which was recovered by Lions linebacker Ernie Sims, led to a 30-yard field goal by Jason Hanson. The Vikings appeared out of sync on offense after that, going three-and-out on their next three possessions as Detroit sent several blitzes at Favre. The Lions, meanwhile, found success in a most surprising way. Detroit had 94 yards rushing, including 48 by running back Kevin Smith, in the first 30 minutes. That figure shrunk to 35 yards after halftime adjustments.

Favre finally guided the Vikings on a 76-yard, 10-play drive that began with a 22-yard run by Peterson and ended with a 1-yard touchdown pass to tight end Visanthe Shiancoe with 1 minute, 4 seconds left in the half. Favre was 7-for-7 during the drive en route to completing 23 of 27 passes for

155 yards with two touchdowns and a 115.3 passer rating.

The late touchdown cut the Lions' lead to 10-7 and swung the momentum for the first time all afternoon. That was key for the visitors; the announced crowd of 56,269 had become extremely vocal, as fans sensed that in their home opener, the Lions (0-2) might have an opportunity to break a losing streak that dates to their second-to-last game of the 2007 season.

"They had to be feeling pretty good about themselves," Favre said of the Lions. "They should have been. I think they played hard the whole game."

For whatever reason, it's nothing new for the Vikings to have problems with Detroit. The Lions, who have a new coach in Jim Schwartz and turned over 62 percent of their roster, lost their two games to the Vikings last season by a total of six points.

At least the Vikings' victory looked like an easy one to those who didn't watch it. Those who played in it knew better.

"We raised the level (in second half). I guess we're durable," Shiancoe said. "That shows our endurance. But we've got to start faster than that. That is definitely not acceptable. That's our second time with that slow start, and against better teams with more explosive offenses, that's not going to cut it."

2009 Regular Season — Vikings 27/Detroit 13 — September 21, 2009

Peterson fan Favre doesn't mind back seat

Ol' No. 4 promises he won't stop handing -- or throwing -- the ball to his new ally, and he says he's not sure piling up yards is a way to win.

Mark Craig, *StarTribune*

DETROIT - The Lions were dangerously close to resembling an NFL team when young Matthew Stafford threw his first career touchdown pass to give them a 10-0 lead late in the second quarter.

"I was worried," admitted old Brett Favre, which is saying something when you consider Sunday marked his record 271st consecutive regular-season start.

At that point, Favre had thrown only one pass that traveled farther than his shadow. Perhaps in a different era and a cheese-colored helmet, Favre would have seen a two-score deficit against a team with 18 consecutive losses as the green light to start winging the ball downfield to whichever team could get to it first.

So far, that's not the guy Zygi Wilf is paying $12 million to this season. The gunslinger has turned in his six-shooter for a pocket protector, horn-rimmed glasses, a 2-0 record and a lifetime membership to the Adrian Peterson Fan Club.

"I just think he's playing within the system," Vikings coach Brad Childress said.

Huh?

"I see him doing the things that he needs to do," Childress went on to say. "It's not like we put a new chip in his head or anything like that."

You sure about that?

Favre answered Stafford's first touchdown pass with the 466th of his 467. It capped a 10-play, 76-yard drive in which Favre dinked and dunked his way downfield, completing seven of seven passes to five different players for 50 yards, including a 1-yard touchdown to Visanthe Shiancoe. None of the passes traveled farther than 5 yards, and they were spread to two tight ends, two receivers and a running back.

"That was probably the most important drive of the game," said Favre, which is saying something when you consider the 27-13 victory raised his regular-season win total to 171 and his record against the Lions to 26-9.

The drive wasn't as simple as it sounds. On third-and-5, Favre had to quickly step up in the pocket to avoid blitzers and, like an old point guard, dished the ball to a younger pair of legs (Percy Harvin) that took it 10 yards for the first down.

"That drive was just Brett knowing the game," said receiver Sidney Rice, who caught two passes for 23 yards during the drive. "We game-plan for teams depending on what defenses they're going to run. Whatever they give us, Brett will take."

Favre completed a franchise-record 85.2 percent of his passes (23 of 27) but had only 155 yards. He threw only two deep balls. Both came in the second half. Both were incomplete, although one resulted in a Lions penalty for illegal contact.

Favre is completing 77.1 percent of his passes on the season, but he has only 265 yards and a 5.5 average per attempt. The yardage total is the lowest Favre has ever had after two games.

"I know it's not a lot of yards, but it's a lot of completions," Favre said. "That's what I said when I first came in, is that it's about getting the ball into the playmakers' hands."

Favre then gave maybe the best indication in NFL history that passing yards are overrated.

"The only time I've ever thrown for 400 yards in my life, (the Packers) lost," said Favre, referring to a 30-17 loss at Chicago in 1993.

Favre also has reached Week 3 without an interception for only the third time in his career. He

did it 1998 and 1996, the year the Packers won the Super Bowl.

After the game, Harvin indicated the Vikings will throw the ball deeper once Favre gets more familiar with the offense. Childress said Favre already knows the entire offense.

"It's just a matter of if we're getting those up-the-field throws," Childress said. "He's not afraid to cut it loose down the field."

For now, however, Favre says he has no problem sitting in the back seat on a team that's one game better than Chicago and Green Bay in the NFC. Favre appeared to hurt his throwing hand while taking a hard hit late in the fourth quarter but said he's healthy enough to be there for No. 272 on Sunday.

"I got no problems telling you that our offense is based around Adrian Peterson, you know?" Favre said. "Big deal. We're going to hand it to him again next week. We're going to throw it to him."

Asked for a guarantee on that, Favre smiled.

"Yeah," he said. "I promise."

2009 Regular Season — Vikings 27/49ers 24 — September 27, 2009

We've seen him do this before, just not for us

Brett Favre has pulled off that last-minute comeback thing before, often against the Vikings. Today was a bit different. But good.

Jim Souhan, *StarTribune*

On his last play in his first home game as a Viking, a rival franchise's exiled legend threw a last second, game-winning touchdown pass he didn't see on a play he didn't remember practicing to a receiver he had barely met.

This is what it means to be Brett Favre.

This is what it means to have Brett Favre.

This is what it means to watch Brett Favre.

"I was on the sidelines saying, `Be Brett, be Brett, be Brett,'" defensive end Jared Allen said. "The Silver Fox came through."

As a prelude to his grudge match with the Packers and an homage to what he did to the Vikings as a Packer, Favre displayed the agony and the ecstacy of Favre-watching in one long afternoon.

He threw lasers to receivers who didn't know they were open. He threw shotgunned mallards toward grateful defenders. He sprinted downfield to body-block one of the best linebackers alive.

He limped and winced, looking older than pyramid dust, and, just when you started wondering why he ever left the Mississippi ranch with the ornate F on the gate, Favre led the kind of drive the Vikings envisioned when they let him treat them like lovestruck teenagers all summer.

The 49ers had taken a 24-20 lead early in the fourth. The Vikings went three-and-out, then failed on a fourth-and-5 on their next two drives.

On their final drive, they took over on their 20 with 1:29 and no timeouts remaining. "I was thinking, `It's a little too late,'" Favre said. "That's not to say you don't go out and sling it."

The Vikings' offense hadn't scored a touchdown since midway through the first quarter, as the 49ers' physical defense contained Adrian Peterson and battered Favre.

Favre feigned optimism.

"He came into the huddle and said, `We're going to get this done,'" receiver Greg Lewis said.

Favre hit Visanthe Shiancoe for 12, then Sidney Rice for 9. After an incompletion, a short pass to Percy Harvin gave the Vikings a first down at their 41. Favre spiked the ball with 40 seconds left.

On the next play, he rolled left and tried to throw deep down the right sideline for Rice, who caught the ball out of bounds. Then Favre threw to Harvin for 15 yards and spiked it with 16 seconds left.

Instead of lobbing a pass to the end zone, Favre threw short to Bernard Berrian, who stepped out of bounds at the 49ers 32 with 12 seconds remaining.

"I wanted to be able to drill one," Favre said. "It's still hard to make it work, but I thought that was better than laying one up."

He took the next snap, faked left, and rolled right. He dodged one pass-rusher, stepped up in the pocket and unleashed a four-seam fastball toward the back of the end zone just as linebacker Manny Lawson hit him in the back, driving him face-first into the turf.

"I saw the ball flying," center John Sullivan said. "I didn't see who was going to catch it, though."

Favre had spotted a flash of purple in the back of the end zone.

"I didn't know who it was," he said.

It was Lewis, the only player newer to the Vikings roster than Favre, and like him another veteran signed in part because of his relationship with coach Brad Childress.

Lewis had taken three snaps in the game before the final play. Favre had thrown only "a couple of hitch patterns" to Lewis in their practice time together. Lewis described the play he was running as something Favre "drew up in the dirt."

Favre's four-seam fastball hit Lewis in stride, Lewis dragged his feet in bounds, and Favre, still on his belly, heard a familiar roar.

"I was in disbelief," Allen said. "The way the place erupted, that gives you chills. That brings you back to Pop Warner days, to the way you felt back then.

"That man has a little mojo on his side."

A lineman yanked Favre to his feet to celebrate; Favre probably needed the lift. He has taken nine sacks and many more hard hits during his first three games in purple, and when reporters entered the locker room Sunday afternoon he sat alone at his corner stall, still wearing his uniform pants and ankle tape.

His face still red, Favre slowly rubbed his right hand over the cropped grey on his head and chin, looking more like a mourner than the guy who just raised 120,000 hands in the air.

For the 42nd time, Favre had led a fourth-quarter comeback victory. For the first time, Vikings fans didn't need mouthguards to protect their molars when Favre started pumping his fists.

"You can't score," Favre said, "if you don't throw it down there."

Favre leaned heavily on the podium as he talked, saying he was so tired he might just fall down.

"I am wore out," he said.

Imagine if he'd had to watch.

2009 Regular Season — Vikings 27/49ers 24 — September 27, 2009

Simply favrelous

The Vikings' hired gun did the job he was brought in to do, throwing a winning TD pass with two seconds left. The fourth-quarter heroics he's famous for involved an 80-yard drive with no timeouts in the final 1:29.

Judd Zulgad, StarTribune

Brett Favre looked tired and felt even worse late Sunday afternoon as he stood at a lectern inside the Metrodome. "I'm worn out," he said. "Believe me, I could fall (over) right now."

At that point, Favre knew what many in the announced crowd of 63,398 probably felt about a half-hour earlier when he completed a 32-yard last-gasp touchdown pass to wide receiver Greg Lewis on third-and-3 with two seconds remaining, giving the Vikings a 27-24 victory over the San Francisco 49ers.

That scoring strike marked the 43rd time the cardiac quarterback had led his team from a fourth-quarter deficit or tie and left the Vikings atop the NFC North with a 3-0 record heading into next Monday's night matchup against the Green Bay Packers at the Metrodome.

The expectations that will come with that game -- one that will pit Favre against the team from which he bitterly divorced after 16 years together -- will be monumental. Yet, it might be hard to top what transpired Sunday in the Vikings' home opener.

"Just another day at the office," coach Brad Childress said.

For these Vikings, that is getting to be the case, and if it continues, perhaps Childress can begin endorsing antacid tablets.

The Vikings had to rally from a halftime deficit for the third game in a row, but unlike the first two they were not able to pull away in the second half for an easy victory.

"We got a couple of 14-point wins which, to me, aren't real world," Childress said. "That one's real world, what you just saw."

Real world or not, it was wildly entertaining.

Don't look at the score but study the statistics and you will be convinced the Vikings won this one going away. The Vikings outgained the 49ers by 131 yards, held them to 0-for-11 on third downs and had the advantage in time of possession (32 minutes, 9 seconds to 27:51).

San Francisco star running back Frank Gore, coming off a 207-yard performance, was forced to leave after one carry when he aggravated an ankle injury.

Despite that, the 49ers were not only able to stick around in this game but actually took a 24-20 lead with 8:12 left in the fourth quarter when tight end Vernon Davis caught a 20-yard touchdown pass from former Viking Shaun Hill. That came after the Vikings rallied from a 17-13 deficit to take a third-quarter lead on Percy Harvin's 101-yard kickoff return for a touchdown.

"His kickoff return was huge, but we really didn't do anything after that until the end," Favre said.

The Vikings had 201 of their 377 yards in the opening 30 minutes but somehow trailed by one at halftime after Ryan Longwell's 44-yard field goal attempt was blocked by Ray McDonald and returned 59 yards for a touchdown by Nate Clements.

"Honestly, I really feel like we made the game tougher on ourselves," Vikings running back Adrian Peterson said.

That's in part because the Niners' 3-4 defense did a good job of making life difficult for Peterson and Favre. Peterson, who had a career-low 3 yards in a victory over the 49ers as a rookie in 2007,

2009 Regular Season — Vikings 27/49ers 24
September 27, 2009

rushed for a much more respectable 85 yards on 19 plays. However, take away a 35-yard run in the first quarter and Peterson goes from averaging 4.5 yards on 19 carries to 2.8 yards on 18 carries.

Favre, meanwhile, threw for 301 yards with two touchdowns and his first interception of the season. He was sacked twice but also took a few other big hits, leaving him bruised and battered. Asked what was hurting him most after the game, Favre couldn't decide.

"My right foot is sore," he said. "Left knee is a little sore, both shoulders, my neck a little bit. Other than that I'm fine."

In the Vikings' eyes, everything turned out fine because of Favre and Lewis. The two not only combined for the winning score, they also strengthened the argument for every player who thinks training camp is a waste of time -- and that's most of them. Favre ended his retirement and joined the Vikings on Aug. 18 after the team had left Mankato; Lewis was signed just over three weeks ago.

In other words, there is no way the two could have been on the same page when it mattered most. Except they were. The Vikings appeared to be in big trouble after turning over the ball on downs with 1:49 left in the fourth quarter when cornerback Dre Bly nearly intercepted Favre's pass for Harvin.

San Francisco then had running back Glen Coffee run three times for 6 yards while the Vikings used all three of their timeouts to stop the clock.

The Vikings started the winning drive from their own 20 with 1:29 left and had no timeouts. Favre was thinking, "We blew our chances," but he never let on. He proceeded to complete five of nine passes -- twice he spiked the ball to stop the clock -- and put the ball at the 49ers 32 with 12 seconds left. Having been in this situation many times before, Favre knew his best chance was to

use his still-strong right arm to drill the ball into the end zone.

So that's what he did. Favre rolled right, lured 49ers defenders toward him and then Favre let fly and was being smacked to the ground from behind by linebacker Manny Lawson. Lewis, who had been inactive for the first two games, made a leaping catch and managed to keep both toes inbounds.

From the ground, Favre realized it was a touchdown when he heard the crowd roar. And then when he got to the sideline he asked the question: Who the heck caught it?

"I didn't know," Favre said. "I just saw one of our guys streaking across."

Favre is now four games from tying John Elway's record for comebacks from a fourth-quarter deficit or tie. Eight of Favre's masterpieces had come against the Vikings while Favre wore green and gold. Finally, the Vikings could celebrate Favre's late-game heroics rather than bemoan them.

"If anything, that just epitomizes what he's all about, and I'm so glad to be on this side of No. 4," Vikings linebacker Ben Leber said.

2009 Regular Season — Vikings 30/Packers 23 — October 5, 2009

Ready for Favre
Ted Thompson retooled the Packers, and ignored Brett Favre's wishes along the way. Which leads us to Monday's game ...

Mark Craig, StarTribune

GREEN BAY, WIS. - Brett Favre and Ted Thompson bumped heads from Day 1 in Green Bay. Actually, it was Day 68 of Thompson's reign as Packers general manager.

The date was April 23, 2005. The Packers had the 24th pick in the draft after losing to the Vikings 31-17 in an NFC wild-card game at Lambeau Field on Jan. 9, 2005, five days before Thompson was hired.

Favre wanted the first round draft pick to be someone who could help him win another Super Bowl. Thompson drafted Favre's heir apparent, Aaron Rodgers, whose contribution was to be ready when the Favre era ended, at least in Green Bay.

That wasn't the last time Thompson and his future Hall of Fame quarterback would disagree.

Favre wanted the Packers to re-sign veteran guards Marco Rivera and Mike Wahle in 2005. Thompson let both free agents walk as he executed a youth movement along the offensive line.

In 2006, Favre wanted Thompson to hire his buddy Steve Mariucci as head coach. Thompson hired a relative unknown in Mike McCarthy, who never had been a head coach before.

In 2007, Favre wanted the team to trade for Randy Moss. Thompson stuck with the team's conservative approach to acquiring veterans, particularly on offense. Moss went to New England.

We all know how the end came in 2008. Favre announced his retirement. The Packers moved on with Rodgers. Favre changed his mind. After an uncomfortable stretch of he-said, he-said, the Packers traded Favre to the Jets. A year later, the Jets released him, he waffled, finally signed with the Vikings and, well, here we are.

Only one more day and Favre will face the Packers with a will to go 4-0 and a side grudge to settle with Thompson at the Metrodome on "Monday Night Football."

Thompson comes to town with the youngest team in the league for the fourth consecutive season. But that's somewhat deceptive. Although the Packers roster averages 25.7 years of age and 3.8 years of experience, Thompson has maintained experience at key positions, especially on defense.

Nowhere is that more evident than at cornerback, where 34-year-old Al Harris and 32-year-old Charles Woodson have a combined 24 years of NFL experience. Ironically, the quarterback who couldn't talk Thompson into adding a veteran on offense will tangle with Woodson, the NFC Defensive player of the month for September and still Thompson's marquee free-agent acquisition (from 2006).

Favre has only one interception this season, coming last week against San Francisco. The Packers defense is tied for the league lead in interceptions (seven) and takeaways (nine).

Who has the advantage? Favre or the defenders who were teammates of his just two years ago?

"I don't know about him having the advantage toward us," linebacker Nick Barnett said. "We had a whole different (defensive scheme) when he was here."

The Packers switched to a 3-4 defense under new coordinator Dom Capers this year. They blitz more often and they play more zone coverage, which allows defenders more time to watch the

quarterback.

"We're familiar with Brett, but I think anybody who follows the NFL and has been alive for the last 19 years is familiar with Brett Favre," Barnett said. "He'll take risks. He took risks when he was here. Sometimes, it was an interception. Sometimes, it was a game-winning touchdown. We just have to be in position and ready to take advantage when he decides to take one of those risks."

Woodson is tied for the league lead in interceptions (three). Harris has one. So does safety Nick Collins, who said the Packers aren't even focusing specifically on Favre this week.

"There's no advantage one way or the other because Brett is not their entire team," Collins said.

"They got a lot of playmakers that make them go. They got Adrian Peterson. They got Percy Harvin. Brett is not the key guy who makes them the so-called `Powerhouse of the North.' Brett is just a guy."

Outside linebacker Aaron Kampman said the Packers are like most teams in that their priority is Peterson.

"Yeah, Brett playing us is unique, and we all know what happened and the circumstances around him leaving," Kampman said. "But it's just a football game we're preparing for. And not to take anything away from Brett Favre, but I think any team that looks at the Minnesota Vikings looks at Adrian Peterson first."

2009 Regular Season — Vikings 30/Packers 23 — October 5, 2009

Even in purple "Silver Fox" shows he still has golden touch

Jim Souhan, *StarTribune*

On Monday night, Brett Favre took a break from being a riddle wrapped in a mystery inside an enigma.

On this night, Favre became more than a displaced Packer wrapped in an old-school Viking uniform inside a dome that once haunted his dreams.

On "Monday Night Football," in the most anticipated football game in Minnesota in years, Favre reminded a deafening crowd and an immense national audience that he once represented so much more than ponderous summer decisions and cynical career calculations.

In a 30-23 Vikings victory that fans of both teams will remember as long as foam cheeseheads remain nonbiodegradable, Favre confirmed his old franchise's worst fears, evoking memories of his Packers glory days while wearing Viking horns.

Favre turns 40 on Saturday, meaning his first start against the Packers marked his last game as a 30-something. We don't know how long the old boy is going to hold up, but after his miracle finish against the 49ers last week and a Monday night of throwing fastballs against his old squad, we know that the guy his teammates call "The Silver Fox" still possesses the golden touch.

"We're used to Favre-a-palooza now," tight end Visanthe Shiancoe said. "We're engulfed in Favre-a-palooza. It's not even Favre-a-palooza anymore. He's family now."

Favre completed 24 of 31 passes for 271 yards, three touchdowns and no interceptions against the Pack. Even a 20-something Favre couldn't have been much better in the first half, going 14-for-17 for 154 yards and two touchdowns.

He wasn't just hitting receivers in stride -- he was hitting them in the lifeline running along their palms. "We have No. 4 now," receiver Sidney Rice said. "He's a part of us now. He's a huge part of us now. He's running the ship."

He hasn't even rammed into any icebergs as a Viking.

On the first drive of the second half, Favre threw a 31-yard touchdown pass to Bernard Berrian, the deep threat who finally seems to have recovered from his nagging hamstring injury. That gave Favre four vital touchdown passes in a 35-minute stretch of football.

A week after his brilliant 2-minute drill against the 49ers, Favre pulled off another one at the end of the first half against the Packers, zipping a 43-yard pass down the seam to Percy Harvin to set up a touchdown that gave the Vikings a 21-14 lead.

Favre didn't just have his fastball -- he displayed surprising "ups," celebrating his first touchdown pass by leaping into the air to collide with Viking kicker and fellow former Packer Ryan Longwell. He even ran downfield in the second qurter to throw a block, and he leaped into the air for another celebration with Chester Taylor. "I think I did knock Chester down that time," Favre said.

The quickness of his decisions trumped the strength of his arm. That's what Vikings fans have been missing in big games for years -- a quarterback who can read a defense like it was a fast-food menu, and deliver quicker than a pizza guy with a new Camaro and heavy debt.

Before the game, Favre belatedly emerged to warm up wearing the Vikings' old-school uniform chosen for Monday night -- and gaudy pink hi-tops to raise awareness for breast cancer. "I knew it

PURPLE REIGN!

would be a zoo out there," Favre said. And: "I was as nervous as I've ever been."

Packers fans had described seeing Favre in purple as "surreal," and the pink shoes only added to the incongruity.

Those close to the Packers say Favre never bestowed much tutoring or career guidance on Aaron Rodgers, but that wasn't Rodgers' problem -- the Vikings' pass rush was.

Packers fans can take solace in this: Favre, with Adrian Peterson in his backfield and a solid offensive line in front of him, had a much easier task than Rodgers, who was responsible for the entire Packers offense and threw half of his passes with Jared Allen's soggy mullet draped over his face.

The Vikings defense ensured that this night would belong to Favre, the graybeard in the purple jersey and pink shoes.

"It really didn't feel that strange," Favre said.

The man was speaking only for himself. The myth becomes `MNF' mega-event

2009 Regular Season — **Vikings 30/Packers 23** — October 5, 2009

The myth becomes "MNF" mega-event

Jim Souhan, *StarTribune*

This isn't going to actually happen, is it? This must be one of those popular myths, like the Loch Ness Monster and tax reform. This must be one of those events we prepare for because of misguided mass hysteria, like Y2K.

Common sense and shared history tells us that Brett Favre never will don purple and sprint onto the Metrodome turf to play against the Green Bay Packers.

This can't happen. And if it does, we will be lucky to be ensconced in a stadium covered by a dome. That way, when locusts swarm and pigs perform the pregame flyover, we will be safe.

Rumors persist that Favre, the man who made America fall in love with the hamlet of Green Bay all over again, who helped turn Lambeau Field into a modernized shrine to Midwestern football, will face his old team tonight in the Metrodome, providing an emotional peak to an improbably momentous Minnesota sports week.

The Twins drew about 140,000 fans for their weekend series with the Royals, and flew in dozens of franchise dignitaries such as Frank Viola and Gary Gaetti to celebrate what they had long supposed would be their last games in the Metrodome.

The Twins won on Sunday, meaning they will bracket "Monday Night Football" with must-win games. "We'll give Brett the dome," said Twins outfielder Michael Cuddyer, "for a day."

Minnesota fans on Sunday watched the Twins culminate one of the most remarkable baseball comebacks in the history of divisional races. And yet the Twins, with their pomp, circumstance and belated excellence, did not make themselves the Minnesota sports story of the week.

Those huge crowds waved Homer Hankies and offered standing ovations to every Twin who cleanly caught a fly ball, yet they will not be the loudest or most fanatical audience of the week.

The Gophers played their first Big Ten game at beautiful TCF Bank Stadium and managed to limit the Wisconsin horde to a few patches of red in the stands, and yet the Gophers became a mere appetizer on the Twin Cities sports landscape.

The persistently popular Wild opened its season on the road on Saturday night, previewing the home opener set for Tuesday, and the Wild could not be more of an afterthought than it is now, with Favre about to take the field.

In terms of mass appeal, fanaticism, ear-splitting ovations, national attention and historical significance, nothing that happened over the past three days will match what will happen tonight, when Favre finally, officially switches sides.

If you are a Viking fan, you have little choice but to embrace a former enemy and hope that he does not lapse into the kind of performances and behaviors that made the Packers grateful for his departure.

If you are a Packers fan, you have little choice but to root against your franchise's foremost icon, a man who, eventually, will enter the Hall of Fame wearing Green Bay garb.

The NFL celebrates physical conflict. Favre is the rare football player capable of causing internal conflict.

"I'm going to be there, and I'll be wearing my green `We'll never forget you, Brent,' T-shirt,'" said Packers fan Jeff Margolis, who lives in Minneapolis. "I'm going to the game with two Vikings fans and two Packers fans.

"It's going to be very surreal, and more than awkward, to see him run out of that tunnel -- and boo him. Because I will boo him. He's a guy you've watched for 16 years, pretty much my

PURPLE REIGN!

entire adult life. It's a shame that I'm going to boo him, but he went to the rival."

Margolis said he doesn't mind Favre playing for another team. He minds greatly that Favre chose to play for the Vikings.

"It's still so bizarre to see him wearing purple," Margolis said. "I almost can't believe what I'm going to see.

"He showed last week that he's still got it, and Vikings fans were giving me a hard time on Monday. I just said, `See what you missed the last 16 years?' Because it was a pleasure watching him. It was a treat. And to see him wearing purple...."

Margolis finished that thought with words inappropriate for polite company, words that will echo around the Metrodome tonight when Favre finally, officially, switches sides.

2009 Regular Season — Vikings 38/St. Louis 10 — October 11, 2009

Taking the fifth

The Vikings made sure they didn't incriminate themselves against the ragged Rams, boosting their record to 5-0. In a prime situation for a letdown, Minnesota instead won in workmanlike fashion, stealing the ball four times.

Judd Zulgad, StarTribune

ST. LOUIS - The Vikings did not spend much time last week focusing on the fact that, after an emotional victory over Green Bay on Monday, they would be facing the winless Rams on Sunday in the depressed environment of the Edward Jones Dome.

But as coach Brad Childress gathered his players Saturday evening in the team hotel he had a message that also served as a challenge.

"This game was more important than last week's game, and it's more important than next week's game," Childress said. "Just from the standpoint that good teams find a way to play on Monday and come back and play on Sunday. Regardless of short time, regardless of who you're playing, playing in the dome. ... If we are who we say we are, we're going to find out a lot about us in terms of what we do in this game."

Childress' players, to their credit, took the next step in proving themselves to be a good team, cruising to a 38-10 victory over a hapless Rams club that did the Vikings plenty of favors by turning over the ball four times. The victory kept the Vikings (5-0) perfect and continued their best start since they opened 6-0 in 2003. The Rams have dropped 15 in a row, dating to last season.

Perhaps the best reason to believe the Vikings have a chance to be successful is that even though it won't earn any style points Sunday's game marked another occasion in which the Viking won when they were expected to win. The Vikings are 3-0 on the road this season, having beaten Cleveland, Detroit and St. Louis. Those three are a combined 2-13. San Francisco is the only team the Vikings have defeated that is above .500.

"I think it's just a testament to the guys in this locker room," linebacker Ben Leber said. "We're not playing down to anybody's level, and we're always striving to get better no matter who we are playing and we always come out with good intensity, good energy and playing smart and playing hard. That's going to overcome a lot of things."

The Vikings stand to find out just how good they are in the three games leading up to their bye week, as they will play host to Baltimore on Sunday before traveling to play the defending Super Bowl champion Pittsburgh Steelers and then the Packers again. The Ravens will be coming to the Metrodome in a sour mood after losing to Cincinnati by three points on Sunday.

"The next three weeks are going to be a strong test of where we are at," defensive end Jared Allen said.

The Vikings will have plenty to correct after giving up 400 yards (278 passing, 122 rushing) to a Rams offense that was averaging 251.3 yards per game entering Sunday and was ranked 30th in the league. The Vikings have given up 824 yards in the past two games after surrendering 779 yards in the first three victories.

"(We're) just continuing to try to evolve and improve," Childress said when asked where he felt his team stands more than a quarter of the way into the season. "It's not my job to grade them. I grade them on how they play. They've been on the right side of the scoreboard, and that's the name of the game. But there's always clean-up work."

Although the Vikings opened the season with back-to-back 14-point victories over the Browns and Lions, in each of those games they trailed

Purple Reign!

at halftime. Another slow start was not an issue Sunday as the Vikings played before an announced crowd of 60,166 that included plenty of fans dressed in purple.

The Vikings jumped to a 14-0 lead, taking the opening kickoff 80 yards on a drive that ended with Adrian Peterson scoring his first of two touchdowns on a 5-yard run. Quarterback Brett Favre established an early tempo with Percy Harvin, connecting with the rookie receiver for a 22-yard gain on third-and-8 and a 24-yarder on second-and-9 from the Rams 29.

St. Louis then started at its own 20-yard line and moved to the Vikings 35. But at that point the Rams began to show their self-destructive ways. Kyle Boller, starting a second consecutive game in place of Marc Bulger at quarterback, lost the ball as he attempted a pass, and Allen picked it up and raced 52 yards for his first career touchdown on defense.

The Rams ended up committing three turnovers inside the Vikings 10-yard line.

Favre, who had the first 5-0 start of his 19-year career, has told his teammates before that from a talent level this is the best team he's ever played on.

"It hasn't come without adversity, and we'll continue to face adversity week in and week out," Favre said "It's not how you start, it's how you finish. But it's important to start fast. There's no doubt, I think anyone who watches us, guys in that room, that we can be a lot better in all three phases.

"Specifically offensively. We go right down the field and score. We struggle to move the ball for the most part until the end. That just proves that there is a lot of areas to improve on. If we do that, just improve in a few areas each week, how good we can be. Now, it only gets tougher from here on out. We know that. But it's a good start."

2009 Regular Season — Vikings 33/Baltimore 31 — October 18, 2009

Lucky left hook

The Vikings remained unbeaten when Steve Hauschka missed a 44-yard field-goal attempt as time expired. Baltimore scored three fourth-quarter touchdowns to take the lead before Sidney Rice made another big play.

Jim Souhan, StarTribune

Reactions on the Vikings side were varied Sunday moments after a 44-yard field-goal attempt by Steve Hauschka sailed wide left with no time remaining, preserving a 33-31 victory over the Baltimore Ravens that was made far more difficult than it should have been.

Quarterback Brett Favre, who couldn't stand to watch, grabbed his helmet with both hands in disbelief. Wide receiver Sidney Rice, coming off the best game of his three-year career, wound up at the other end of the field, appearing to give thanks as he crouched on his hands and knees on the Metrodome turf.

Defensive end Jared Allen -- who was among a large group unimpressed with how his team finished -- put aside any frustration, at least for a moment. "Absolutely relieved," he said when asked to express his emotions. "You get disgusted if you lose that game. Sometimes it's better to be lucky than good. You look at that fourth quarter and you say there is no way this is the same team that was playing the first three quarters. We had a little wake-up call. You've got to keep playing."

The Vikings seemed to forget this as the Ravens came storming back to score 21 points in the final quarter and for 15 minutes looked like an offensive juggernaut.

This doesn't mean the Vikings are about to make any apologies. They are off to a 6-0 start for the first time since 2003 and the sixth time in franchise history. That is the best record in the NFL -- New Orleans and Indianapolis are 5-0 -- although Denver could equal the Vikings' mark tonight by winning at San Diego.

But even the Vikings have to know they are extremely lucky to still be perfect. Favre engineered a last-second drive in a 27-24 victory over San Francisco in Week 3 and again worked his magic Sunday in a game in which the Vikings had appeared poised to run away with early on.

"We were fortunate to win that game, and we were fortunate to beat San Francisco," Favre said. "I have no idea what will happen in the future. That's what I tried to tell some of the guys.

"(Linebacker) Chad Greenway and I walked up the tunnel together. The type of guy he is, he was disappointed. He was looking at the negative. I said, `Hey, maybe next week just the opposite. You guys (on defense) will have to pull it out for us.' But that's not to say there's things you can't improve on."

The mistakes that will need to be cleaned up today in film review, especially from the defensive standpoint, won't be the Vikings' only concerns. Pro Bowl cornerback Antoine Winfield suffered an injury to his right foot in the first half that ended his day, and rookie receiver Percy Harvin re-injured his left shoulder on a fourth-quarter kickoff return. There also was a scary moment when Adrian Peterson limped off the field in the fourth quarter after being twisted awkwardly as he was tackled, but the Pro Bowl running back was able to return.

As much as the Vikings would like to focus on the things they did right Sunday in handing the Ravens a third consecutive loss -- touchdowns on their first two drives gave the Vikings a 14-0 lead, the Ravens rushed for 13 yards in the first half -- they are going to have to take a good long look at the fourth quarter.

It isn't going to be pretty.

The Ravens accumulated 222 of their 448 yards in the final 15 minutes, including 196 passing

2009 Regular Season — Vikings 33/Baltimore 31
October 18, 2009

yards by quarterback Joe Flacco. The Ravens' yardage total was a season-high against the Vikings and marked the third game in a row they have surrendered 400 or more yards. Flacco finished with 385 yards passing, 1 more than the total Aaron Rodgers had in Week 4 when the Packers put together a fourth-quarter rally.

Some of Sunday's meltdown had to do with the fact that with Winfield not on the field, Flacco went at his replacement, Karl Paymah, on a regular basis. The Ravens trailed 27-10 with 10 minutes, 8 seconds left and by 13 with 6:01 to go but managed to take a 31-30 lead when running back Ray Rice sliced through the defense for a 33-yard touchdown with 3:37 remaining.

There appeared to be a level of panic on the Vikings sideline, but Favre provided his usual calming influence. A 58-yard completion to Sidney Rice -- a play in which the receiver made a spectacular catch despite being interfered with by cornerback Frank Walker -- set up Ryan Longwell's 31-yard field goal that gave the Vikings a two-point lead with 1:56 to play.

However, starting at his own 33-yard line with no timeouts, Flacco continued to have his way with the Vikings defense. He advanced Baltimore to the Vikings 29 on the strength of four completions on seven attempts. Rice then gained 3 yards before Flacco spiked the ball on third down to set up Hauschka's attempt.

Hauschka spent 2008 training camp with the Vikings and had the ultimate chance to get some revenge. It didn't happen that way. Vikings coach Brad Childress first attempted to ice Hauschka by calling time right before his attempt -- "I will admit that I second-guessed myself when (Hauschka) stumbled on the way to the kick before they got the timeout in," Childress said -- and then celebrated along with his players and an announced crowd of 63,689 as the kick sailed wide.

"I thought I hit it pretty good on my foot," Hauschka said. "I looked up and it was going left, so I was disappointed."

As for Childress' emotions? Well, it turns out there was never a doubt in his mind that his team would prevail. At least that's what he told Peterson as they stood on the sideline right before Hauschka's kick.

"I just told him we were going to win this football game right here," Childress said. "And that crowd over there (the Ravens) had a heart of a champion to fight back and get it where they got it to. We've got that same heart. We just need to learn how to finish."

2009 Regular Season — Vikings 33/Baltimore 31 — October 19, 2009

Rice finds success in being on the same wavelength as Favre

The third-year receiver piled up 176 yards by making adjustments and trusting in his veteran quarterback.

Mark Craig, StarTribune

The chemistry between Brett Favre and Sidney Rice appears to becoming along nicely, considering it produced two of the biggest plays in Sunday's 33-31 victory over the Ravens at the Metrodome.

The 63-yard reception that set up Ryan Longwell's third-quarter field goal came on a play that Favre changed from run to pass. And the 58-yarder that led to Longwell's game-winner late in the fourth quarter came on a play in which Rice changed his route while trusting that Favre would understand why, which, of course, he did.

On the 58-yarder, Rice was supposed to run a 12- to 15-yard comeback route. When he saw an advantage in man coverage with cornerback Frank Walker, he changed to a go route.

Favre spotted the same advantage, bought enough time in the pocket to set up for a deeper throw and launched a ball that wasn't pretty but sufficed. Despite Walker grabbing his jersey for several steps downfield, Rice caught the ball and was downed at the Baltimore 18.

"That's the type of plays (Rice) can make," Favre said. "Sometimes, you have to adjust. He just felt like he had the advantage. We have had that discussion in the past, that if he feels like he can get on top, or can win, then do it."

Rice caught six passes for 176 yards (29.3-yard average). It tied his career high for receptions and was a career high for yardage by 94 yards. It also is the ninth-best receiving total in team history.

"He's having a nice year and I think it's fun," offensive coordinator Darrell Bevell said of the third-year receiver. "I think we're having a good time. I think the guys all feel part of it, which is exciting for me. They feel like they all have a piece.

I've got the linemen yelling at me to run it, I've got the receivers yelling at me to throw it and this guy wants a ball, that guy wants a ball. It's fun because they all feel like they have a part in this thing."

Favre threw to eight different receivers, completing at least one pass to seven of them. Rice's 63-yard reception was high for the game and his career.

Not bad, considering Rice didn't think the ball was coming his way.

"I didn't think he had changed the play," Rice said. "When I seen the safety pass my face, I kind of looked in and that's when he let the ball go. Hit me right in the chest and I was able dodge a couple defenders and get to the sideline."

Just another step in the evolution of Favre and his Purple receivers.

"He distributes the ball to everyone," Rice said. "Everybody gets their touches. Nobody is complaining. Everybody is happy with 6-0, and it's great."

2009 Regular Season — **Vikings 33/Baltimore 31** — October 19, 2009

Improvisation a QB quality we're unfamiliar with here

Jim Souhan, StarTribune

If the Vikings ever get a chance to remodel the Metrodome to suit their needs, before they add luxury suites and VIP seats, before they plaster ads on the walls and hang a papier-mache homage to Brad Childress' beard from the Teflon roof, they need to make one simple alteration to suit their new quarterback.

Along the sideline, the Vikings need to add a patch of dirt, so Brett Favre will have a place to draw his game-winning plays.

Whatever doubts we had about the terms of his arrival or the prospects of his durability, Favre today stands as the difference between 6-0 and 4-2, if not abject mediocrity.

After improvising a long pass to Sidney Rice that set up what would prove to be the winning field goal in a 33-31 victory over Baltimore on Sunday, Favre has won two games with plays remodeled to suit his whim and his receivers' instincts, plays that previous quarterbacks under Childress would not have had the authority or guts to call, plays that worked because under pressure Favre becomes as much a cousin of John Coltrane as Johnny Unitas.

To beat the 49ers on a last-second touchdown pass Sept. 27, Favre rolled right, stepped up in the pocket and took a crunching hit while throwing to a flash of purple in the back of the end zone that turned out to be receiver Greg Lewis, to whom Favre had never previously completed a pass.

To beat the Ravens on Sunday, Favre checked out of a running play, rolled right, ignored the primary receiver, stepped up in the pocket because he saw Sidney Rice fighting off a single defensive back, and threw a pass that the author of the play would not have imagined.

Rice's 58-yard catch led to the final points of the game, leaving Childress to meander toward a vague reference to the "Hound of the Baskervilles" in his postgame news conference, and Favre to admit that, when time is tight, his creativity becomes unloosed.

"He was supposed to have a 12- or 15-yard comeback, I think," Favre said of Rice. "Sometimes, you have to adjust."

Before Favre hitched a ride with him from the airport, Childress seemed more likely to appear on "Dancing With The Stars" than to tolerate an audible. He antagonized smart, veteran quarterbacks such as Brad Johnson, Kelly Holcomb and Gus Frerotte with his inflexibility.

Now, after every game, Favre describes plays like his 1-yard touchdown pass to Visanthe Shiancoe on Sunday: "That was actually not the formation or personnel we wanted. We almost called timeout. I knew by Fahu's look (Naufahu Tahi) that he had no clue.

"He hadn't run that play. You just have to be able to adapt sometimes."

Before Favre arrived, who would have envisioned this exchange between a quarterback and Childress on the sideline during a close game?

Childress: "We need to stay on the gas right here."

Favre: "No (kidding), Sherlock."

Recounting the conversation, Favre grinned and Childress made his obscure literary reference of the day, to Arthur Conan Doyle's Holmes vehicle, "Hound of the Baskervilles."

The Vikings' unbeaten record is no mystery. Favre has thrown 12 touchdown passes. He has thrown two interceptions. He has yet to lose a fumble. He has led two late-game comebacks.

He has completed 69.7 percent of his passes. The Vikings have scored at least 27 points in every game Favre has started.

Past performances may not be indicative of future results, but Favre appears to have at least attempted to quell questions about his worth as a teammate, after he left the Packers and Jets cold.

"He is just a great guy, all-around," Rice said. "You hear all of the talk from the past teams that he has been on. We don't see it at all. He is communicating with us, and talking to us.

"He is sitting down and watching film with the receivers, extra film and things like that. It is great to have a leader on your team like that. He has been in the game for a very long time and you can learn so much from a guy like that."

After the Vikings blew a 17-point lead and won only because of a missed last-second field goal, we could question the defense and second-guess strategy, but the Vikings are 6-0, Childress is taking grief from and ceding control to his quarterback, and we are enjoying the privilege of watching Favre improvise like Charlie Parker in a smoke-filled room.

2009 Regular Season   Steelers 27/Vikings 17   October 25, 2009

Burghlary victims
With team on the move, Favre magic is taken away

Judd Zulgad, *StarTribune*

PITTSBURGH - After a day filled with too many penalties and what seemed like countless missed opportunities, the Vikings were left with one thing as they assumed possession of the football at their own 26 with 3 minutes, 21 seconds left in the fourth quarter Sunday at Heinz Field.

Hope.

Trailing by three points, the Vikings had one of the NFL's greatest weapons when it comes to late-game rallies. Brett Favre had directed teams from a fourth-quarter deficit or tie 44 times in his 19-year career, including twice this season. There was little reason to believe it wouldn't happen again.

"Everybody's mindset on the sideline was, 'We're going to win this game. We don't know how we're going to do it but we're going to win this game,' " linebacker Ben Leber said.

That belief probably existed beyond the visitors' sideline as Favre drove the Vikings to the Steelers' 19 with 1:15 left. But for at least one day the magic disappeared. Favre's screen pass on second down sailed a bit high and running back Chester Taylor deflected it into the waiting hands of Steelers linebacker Keyaron Fox.

Fox returned the ball 82 yards for a touchdown, giving Pittsburgh a 27-17 victory and handing the Vikings their first loss of the season after six victories. Steelers coach Mike Tomlin gained a victory over Brad Childress, the guy who he spent a season working for as the Vikings' defensive coordinator in 2006.

Perhaps it was fitting then that the Steelers defense, a group directed by one of the NFL's all-time great coordinators in Dick LeBeau, scored 14 points off turnovers. Pittsburgh's aggressive 3-4 scheme also held Adrian Peterson to 69 yards on 18 carries, the fifth time this season an opponent has managed to hold the Pro Bowl running back to fewer than 100 yards rushing.

Afterward there wasn't a feeling of anger in the Vikings locker room -- an NFC North-leading 6-1 record with the loss coming to an out-of-conference opponent isn't exactly reason to be alarmed -- but there was definitely a realization that this team had lost a very winnable road game.

It also might have lost a valuable receiver: Bernard Berrian spent the second half as a spectator after appearing to injure his left hamstring. Berrian refused to discuss the injury afterward.

"We gave them the game but hats off to them," tight end Visanthe Shiancoe said. "They are a good defense, and they are a good team overall. They capitalized on mistakes that we made, that we shouldn't have made and that's the way the game just went."

Among the most glaring issues for the Vikings were penalties. A week after being called for only three infractions in a victory over Baltimore, the Vikings committed a season-high 11 Sunday. This included a crucial tripping call on Vikings tight end Jeff Dugan in the fourth quarter that wiped out a 10-yard touchdown pass to Sidney Rice. That would have given the Vikings a 17-13 lead.

Instead, three plays later, Favre was stripped of the ball on a sack and Steelers linebacker LaMarr Woodley returned the fumble 77 yards, giving Pittsburgh a 10-point cushion.

That turned out to be a good thing for the Steelers when Percy Harvin returned the ensuing kickoff 88 yards for a touchdown, making him the first player in Vikings history to have two kick returns for a score in one season.

2009 Regular Season — Steelers 27/Vikings 17
October 25, 2009

At that point it became obvious that while execution might be an issue for the Vikings, resiliency certainly was not.

"I'm proud of my guys for fighting back," Vikings coach Brad Childress said. "I hate the result, but I thought they put themselves in position to win that football game. Hats off to [the Steelers]. They found a way to make a couple plays."

This included a touchdown late in the first half that Pittsburgh quarterback Ben Roethlisberger orchestrated in a very Favre-like 1:15. The eight-play, 91-yard effort ended with Roethlisberger completing a pass to Mike Wallace in which the speedy receiver was able to avoid safety Madieu William en route to the end zone. That turned a four-point Steelers deficit into a three-point lead and marked the last time Pittsburgh trailed.

The Vikings were left to lament the fact that both safety Tyrell Johnson and linebacker E.J. Henderson had their hands on Roethlisberger passes during that drive.

The Vikings had a chance to take a 14-13 lead in the third quarter when Favre's 34-yard pass to Rice on fourth-and-1 put the ball at the Steelers' 1. But after Peterson was stopped for no gain and Favre's passes fell incomplete for Rice and Kleinsasser on second and third down, Ryan Longwell came on to make an 18-yard field goal.

"I just thought it was important to take the points there," Childress said when asked if he considered going for it again. "They kind of nubbed us there. I think we had one play and they were offsides [on first down] and we really had four downs."

Although Favre certainly wouldn't agree, the game might have come to a fitting end when Steelers linebacker James Harrison slammed the quarterback to the ground, giving Pittsburgh its fourth sack of the day and fifth victory of the season.

"We answered the call for the most part, we just didn't make enough plays," Favre said. "You always feel better after a game like this if you win, and unfortunately we didn't win it."

2009 Regular Season Steelers 27/Vikings 17 October 25, 2009

Vikings look better losing than winning
Jim Souhan, StarTribune

PITTSBURGH - The Vikings' weekend trip to Pittsburgh reportedly started with Brad Childress donning lipstick, heels and a stewardess outfit on the team charter. It ended with an even better reason to seek therapy.

His team committed a series of devastating penalties and turnovers, and the game ended with Brett Favre coccooned under 242 pounds of ham hocks and gristle named James Harrison.

In an eight-minute stretch of the fourth quarter, two Favre turnovers turned into defensive scores for the Steelers, and a tripping penalty wiped out a Vikings touchdown. By the end of the Steelers' 27-17 victory at picturesque Heinz Field, you almost wish you had glimpsed Childress in drag, just so the temporary blindness would save you from seeing Favre feigning interest in making a tackle in the open field.

If you can accept the random nature of the events that decided the game, though, and study what actually happened in the second half, you realize that the Vikings might be more impressive at 6-1 than they were at 6-0.

On spotty sod in one of the most intimidating NFL stadiums while facing a varied and fierce defense led by legendary coordinator Dick LeBeau and amid the kind of cacophony that can make you forget your own name, Favre led the kind of drives to which we are not accustomed, drives filled with creativity and grit, drives that easily could have won the toughest game on the 2009 schedule.

"I love the way we competed," Favre said. "I knew it would be tough. I knew when I decided to come here, I looked at our schedule and said, 'Wooo.'"

The Steelers took a 13-7 lead with a field goal on their first drive of the second half. From that point, the Vikings dominated the play from scrimmage against the defending Super Bowl champs.

Here's what happened the last five times the Vikings touched the ball:

They drove 64 yards to the Steelers' 1 before settling for a field goal. (I would have given the ball to Adrian Peterson, but that decision didn't decide the game.)

They went three-and-out after a false start penalty -- and after a perfect pass from Favre fell incomplete when Percy Harvin took a crushing hit deep downfield.

On their first drive of the fourth quarter, the Vikings started on their 3 and drove to the Pittsburgh 8. From the 10, Favre's touchdown pass to Sidney Rice was nullified by a tripping call on Jeff Dugan that enraged the Vikings staff. On third-and-goal from the 8, Favre had the ball knocked from his hand, and LaMarr Woodley ran 77 yards for a touchdown. A Vikings field goal would have made it 13-13; a touchdown would have given them the lead against a team struggling to move the ball.

On the next kickoff, Harvin sprinted 88 yards for a touchdown, making it 20-17.

After the Vikings forced a punt and took over at their 26, Favre drove them to the Pittsburgh 19. On second-and-3, Favre's screen pass zipped through Chester Taylor's hands. Keyaron Fox caught the deflection and ran for a touchdown with Favre wisely performing a hook slide at midfield to avoid contact.

On their last drive of the game, with time running out, Favre drove the Vikings from their 37 to the Pittsburgh 19 before Harrison embedded Favre in the sod.

To summarize: Facing the defending champs on their home field, the Vikings amassed 264 yards in the second half, as Favre, Peterson and Rice played like champions.

With the Steelers limiting his space in the running game, Peterson caught three passes for 59 yards in the game's last nine minutes, once flattening cornerback William Gay in the open field. Favre threw 51 passes, completing 34 for 334 yards, while facing the Steelers' unpredictable blitzes and brutal hits.

"Those two are always fighting hard," kicker Ryan Longwell said of Peterson and Favre. "With them, you're never out of a game. There is no quit in either of them. When you have them on your side, you can do a lot of things."

Victories can obscure flaws; losses can reveal quality. At the end of this loss, one could look around the league and recognize that, for the moment, the Vikings employ the best running back/quarterback combination in the NFL. Even if Favre can't tackle.

2009 Regular Season
November 1, 2009

They can't believe it in Green Bay: Favre lives!
Emotions will run high when a purple-clad Brett Favre steps onto Lambeau Field.
Judd Zulgad, StarTribune

Ken Carriveau didn't think a master's degree in counseling would do him much good five years ago when he took over the Stadium Sports and Memorabilia store near Lambeau Field.

But now there are days when Carriveau feels more like a confidant to his customers than the proprietor of a Packers merchandise shop.

"I have regulars that come in, and it's where they come to vent and talk," he said. "I have guys that come in and don't even look to buy anything. They've never even thought about buying anything, but they'll come and spend three hours talking."

The subject is always Brett Favre.

The future Hall of Fame quarterback built his legend during 16 seasons as a Packer and will return today for the first time as a member of the archrival Vikings. Many grown Wisconsin men wrestle with that the same way a young girl might struggle with the fact that Kevin Jonas isn't waiting to marry her.

There was a mock funeral. Disparaging T-shirts are for sale all around town. The hooting about Favre will fill the air along with the smoke from grilled bratwurst today as the tailgaters crack open their beers in the festive atmosphere around the historic stadium.

This wasn't how things were supposed to work. Not for their quarterback. It was tough seeing him wear a New York Jets jersey last season ... but to see him run out of the visitor's tunnel at Lambeau Field in a Vikings uniform? Unthinkable.

So they bare their souls to Carriveau. And then they talk some more.

"Nobody knows who to get behind," said Carriveau, 63, a lifelong Packers fan and still a Favre supporter. "Everybody is so still enmeshed in the mix of, 'Who is to blame?'

"It's like, 'Get over it. The guy has been gone for 20 months.' ... I think they have to let go. It's like a bad divorce. They have to stop taking sides."

The blame game

Favre's separation from the Packers did play out like a celebrity divorce. Feeling pressured, Favre retired in March 2008 before changing his mind months later and deciding he wanted to return.

The Packers told him they had moved on with young quarterback Aaron Rodgers. Things escalated until Favre was traded to the Jets that August. His desire had been to play for the Vikings, but there was no way Packers General Manager Ted Thompson was going to let that happen.

Caught in the middle were Packers fans, many of whom couldn't remember another quarterback starting a game for the franchise.

The division on how people feel -- many are convinced he has committed football treason by joining the Vikings, while others will never forgive the Packers -- is why no one knows what to expect when he does take the field today. A cascade of boos and catcalls? A mix of boos and cheers? A polite ovation when he enters and boos once the game begins?

Angst is easy to spot

Brett Favre's Steakhouse is not far from Carriveau's store and is reached by turning from Holmgren Way -- named after Mike Holmgren, who coached Favre and the Packers to a Super Bowl victory after the 1996 season -- onto Brett Favre Pass. Only some enterprising soul turned the last word of the street into an off-color term by covering up a key letter. On the same day that bit of

artistic work was spotted by a reporter, two women were taking pictures of each other in front of a Favre-related monument.

Then there is the radio station that sponsored a Funeral-4-Favre at a bar near Lambeau this weekend.

So what will happen today? That is anyone's guess.

But some simply won't be able to watch.

Bill Wenzel, the president of Fuzzy Thurston's Titletown Ticket and Tours, began buying tickets to this game after Favre signed with the Vikings in mid-August.

"A lot of Packers fans, I just think their stomach is turned by the fact that Brett Favre will be running around in our house in a purple uniform," said Wenzel, 53. "A lot of people come in and say they don't want to be any part of that."

Wenzel's office is adjacent to Fuzzy's Bar and Grill, a business named after the longtime Packers guard. Thurston's son, Mark, is the bar's general manager. He hasn't decided the proper way to greet Favre.

"I'm not going to boo," said Mark Thurston, 51. "I can't cheer for him, either. He's a Minnesota Viking, and I don't like the Vikings whether he was on the team or not. There's a lot of people like that, too."

Mark Thurston said that his parents were both "very disappointed" to see Favre join the Vikings and that his mom, Sue, has taken down photos of the quarterback that used to hang on the walls of his parents' home. "They didn't throw them away or anything like that," Mark said. "But she had some prominently displayed ones. I think they got moved."

Fuzzy's Bar and Grill is decorated with photos from yesteryear -- Fuzzy played for the Packers from 1959-67 -- and there are a few of Favre. There also are Favre shirts for sale, but none of them flattering. One says "We'll never forget you, BRENT." Another says "Thanks 4," on the front and "nothing" on the back.

Nothing like a little humor to dull the pain.

Purple preview?

Dave Pearson, a native of Hayward, Wis., and lifelong Packers fan, plans to watch today's game a few miles from Lambeau -- from the house in which Favre lived with his wife, Deanna, and daughters Brittany and Breleigh.

Pearson, an engineering supervisor at the Point Beach nuclear power plant southeast of Green Bay, closed on the house on Shady Lane last November when he, his wife, Sunny, and 7-year-old daughter Amanda returned to Wisconsin after 10 years in Virginia. Pearson never dealt with Brett, but he did get to meet Deanna -- the house was in her name -- and calls her a "wonderful lady."

Perhaps that's why Pearson is rooting for Favre to do his best today -- in a loss. "I would like to see him throw for over 400 yards and lose the game," Pearson said. "There's precedent there because the only other time he threw for over 400 yards was in '93. I believe it was against the Bears and the Packers lost 30-17."

PURPLE REIGN!

Pearson, 45, said that when he first saw the house there was little that would have alerted anyone that one of the NFL's all-time great quarterbacks lived there. But a few months ago he did make an interesting discovery.

Pearson found two cans of paint in the basement. One was for a Wales Green mix. The other gallon is marked "potentially purple." In fact, Pearson provided a tour of the house and pointed out that Brittany's room was painted purple.

"It was funny," Pearson said of finding the paint.

Forgiveness? Forget it

But many don't have a sense of humor when it comes to Favre-related topics. One man's funny is another's proof that Favre turned out to be nothing more than a traitor.

Carriveau urges his patients, er, customers not to feel this way, but admits it can be difficult to know how to feel. He tells the story of a friend who is a Packers shareholder, yet has given his season tickets to others to use and has purchased Vikings season tickets.

"I feel like I've lost a family member, and it's almost like you need to go through a funeral or something," Carriveau said of the loss of Favre. "Some rite of passage that allows you to say, 'OK, it's done, it's over.'

"Packers fans haven't done that for the most part. There are a few of us that have and just said, 'Remember the best, forget the rest and move on.' "

A few. But not many. As Favre may find out today.

2009 Regular Season   Vikings 38/Packers 26   November 1, 2009

Longwell sees clearly why focus is on friend Favre
No. 4's new teammate and old friend hadn't won in purple at Lambeau since the quarterback had left. This was a good day to be on the same side again.

Jim Souhan, *StarTribune*

GREEN BAY, WIS. - Brett Favre had just thrown four touchdown passes to beat the Packers, had celebrated with new teammates and consoled old friends, had choked up as he talked on the turf at fast-emptying Lambeau Field. Now Favre and the cameras attached to him like suckerfish to a shark drifted toward the end zone, where a new teammate and old friend waited.

Ryan Longwell made the transfer from Packers green to Vikings purple three years before Favre. They had talked in June, months before Favre actually signed with the Vikings, about returning to Lambeau together.

Now Longwell was parting the cameras and hugging Favre, telling him, "I'm proud of you," and Favre was throwing one arm around Longwell's neck and the other into the air as he jogged into the tunnel.

How many times had Favre executed the famous Lambeau Leap, vaulting into the stands to celebrate a touchdown? Now, after beating the Packers 38-26 in the most-anticipated midseason NFL game in memory, Favre was weeping instead of leaping.

"We got it," Favre said to Longwell.

"I'm so happy for you," Longwell said to Favre.

Longwell had not won in Green Bay as a Viking, not until Favre, in front of a Lambeau regular-season record crowd of 71,213, completed 17 of 28 passes for 244 yards, with four touchdowns, no interceptions and no sacks.

What could be worse for Packers fans, than to lose to the player they revere and revile, in the stadium he helped renovate? "This ranks high," Favre said.

In two games against the Packers, Favre is 2-0 with seven touchdowns, no interceptions and no sacks. Sunday, he led the Vikings to a 24-3 lead early in the third quarter, and the game might have turned into a blowout if not for defensive end Brian Robison fumbling away a kickoff return midway through that quarter.

With Lambeau swaying, the Packers rallied to within 24-20 and 31-26 before Favre ended the drama with a 16-yard touchdown pass to Bernard Berrian with 3:48 remaining.

Favre not only buried the Packers -- the Vikings now have a 2 1/2-game lead and a tiebreaking advantage over Green Bay with eight games left -- he again outplayed his replacement, Aaron Rodgers, who threw for more yards (287) but took six sacks and looked tentative during some of the game's biggest moments.

As time ran out, Favre walked slowly onto the field with his head down and his fists high. He sought out former teammates Donald Driver, Greg Jennings and Rodgers, and his former coach, Mike McCarthy.

Favre's departure from Green Bay turned ugly when McCarthy and Packers General Manager Ted Thompson tired of Favre's indecisiveness over retirement. Sunday, Favre seemed intent on avoiding any gestures that could have been interpreted as taunts.

"I told him, 'Way to battle, good to see you, good luck to you,'" Favre said of his brief conversation with McCarthy. "I want to lead this Vikings team to a Super Bowl, believe me, and I'm going to do everything within my power. But I also know that Packer fans will never change. How could you not miss that? ...

"I'm glad it's over. I'm glad we won both. But

I'm not going to sit here and throw any daggers."

He already had carved the Packers secondary with vintage Favre fastballs, already had won the biggest game played in Lambeau since he left.

"Say what you want about Reggie White and the other guys, but Brett brought the Packers back to prominence," Longwell said. "He plays an infectious style of football that you gravitate to. He had every right to take even more satisfaction, especially when they're booing him.

"Brett's playing as well as I've ever seen him. Say what you want about him being 40 years old, but he's in control of the offense and can wing it. The boos were loud, but I was amazed at how fast they went away when it was 24-3."

Earlier in the day, Longwell had spotted a frame store in Green Bay featuring a sign reading: "Welcome back, Ryan Longwell."

The frame store didn't offer any such sentiments to Favre, but by Sunday night, Packers fans had gotten the picture.

2009 Regular Season — Vikings 38 / Packers 27
November 1, 2009

Lord of Lambeau

If 71,213 booing Packers fans vociferously disagreed, the former Packers great was dazzling in his return, throwing for four touchdowns with no interceptions.

Judd Zulgad, *StarTribune*

GREEN BAY, WIS. - Brett Favre wasn't sure he agreed with the sentiment, but he heard the same message on multiple occasions over the weekend as he prepared to play his first game in Lambeau Field as a visitor.

"I can't tell you how many text messages or guys just in passing today and yesterday [said], 'Hey, you're going to play great. I know you're nervous,' " Favre said. "I'm like, 'It's easy for you to say.' But they were right again."

Indeed, they were. Favre, whose Hall of Fame resume has been built on winning some pressure-filled games, did it again Sunday, throwing four touchdown passes with no interceptions in a 38-26 victory over the Packers. In doing so Favre helped the Vikings complete a series sweep of the Packers and again proved to Green Bay General Manager Ted Thompson and coach Mike McCarthy that he still had plenty of life left in that right arm that was no longer desired in these parts after 16 years.

That bitter divorce is what made Sunday's matchup so intriguing and actually buried the story line that this game was of huge importance in the NFC North race.

Favre was met with a chorus of thundering boos from disapproving fans in the crowd of 71,213 -- the largest for a regular season game in Lambeau Field history -- as he entered the field before the kickoff. Many of those fans had warmed up by booing Favre earlier when he came out about a half-hour before kickoff to warm up.

What Green Bay fans quickly learned is what Vikings fans knew for so many years: Favre is a pain to play against. His performance Sunday and throughout the season is a big reason the Vikings will head into their bye week in control of the NFC North with a 7-1 record. That mark gives them a 2 1/2-game lead over the Packers (4-3) and Chicago (4-3). The Vikings also have the tiebreaker on Green Bay because they swept the series.

"It's huge. This is all we could ask for going into the bye," defensive end Jared Allen said of being 7-1. "We're exactly where we want to be. We're ahead in the division going into the bye week. This is a team that continues to learn from our victories and from our losses."

Favre finished with seven touchdown passes, no interceptions and 515 yards passing in two victories against his old team. He also wasn't sacked in either game. The Vikings defense, meanwhile, sacked Favre's successor, Aaron Rodgers, six times on Sunday and 14 times in the two meetings. Allen had three sacks on Sunday and has 7 1/2 of his 10 1/2 against Green Bay.

The Vikings had not swept both games from the Packers since 2005, and Sunday's victory was coach Brad Childress' first in Lambeau Field after three losses. The Vikings also have won three in a row over the Packers after Childress lost his first five against McCarthy. The first four, of course, were orchestrated by Favre when he was a hero to the Lambeau faithful and not the pariah he has become.

Childress said Favre did a good job of controlling his emotions and aside from an unexpected shotgun snap that center John Sullivan delivered in the first quarter, which resulted in a turnover that led to a Packers field goal, there were few mistakes. "We talked a little bit about not doing too much," Childress said. "You have a tendency to do too much sometimes, and I thought

2009 Regular Season — Vikings 38/Packers 27
November 1, 2009

he did just about what he needed to do. He didn't get too creative or try to rig anything up. I just thought he kept it in body, didn't get out of body."

As he stood in the cramped visitor's interview room Sunday, Favre again swore the fact he is now having success as a member of the Packers' arch-rival isn't about revenge.

"Am I pleased with the way these two games have turned out? Absolutely," he said. "It had nothing to do with trying to prove myself to anyone. I still have a passion for it. It's a little bit tougher to get up and bounce back but my arm feels great. My mind is in a good place, the team has welcomed me in and really all the other stuff doesn't matter. I know it makes for a good story. But I'm glad it's over, I'm glad we won both but I'm not going to sit here and throw any daggers."

Favre didn't need to, considering he and his teammates had done that on the field, although they made things far more interesting than was necessary. The Vikings appeared to be set to embarrass the Packers when Percy Harvin caught a 51-yard touchdown pass that Favre put into triple coverage, making it 24-3 early in the third quarter. The Packers countered with a field goal. But when Vikings defensive end Brian Robison attempted to run with Mason Crosby's short kickoff, he fumbled the ball and it was recovered by the Packers' Nick Collins at the Vikings 41.

Green Bay, which had 47 yards on offense in the first half but 304 in the second, got back-to-back touchdown passes from Rodgers to tight end Spencer Havner, and it was 24-20 entering the fourth quarter.

But as he had done for much of the day, the explosive Harvin made a big play after that second score. The rookie, who had a 77-yard kickoff return that set up the Vikings' first touchdown, went 48 yards with a return to start a seven-play drive that ended with Favre hitting Jeff Dugan for a 2-yard touchdown. The Packers had a chance to pull within two points in the fourth quarter but Crosby missed a 51-yard field-goal attempt.

Harvin, who had been listed as questionable after missing practice Thursday because of an illness, had five catches for 84 yards with a touchdown and returned five kickoffs for an average of 35 yards. Harvin finished with 261 total yards.

"I hate losing to whoever's at quarterback for them," Rodgers said of having been beaten twice by Favre. "I hate losing to the Vikings, especially. Division rivals. Don't like losing at home. The crowd was electric tonight. Their support was amazing. It kind of carried us through there in the third quarter. We just could not keep that momentum going and couldn't finish off the drive we had to take the lead. That's disappointing. It doesn't matter who you play, though; it's tough to lose."

Favre made it clear when he signed in August that he was coming back because the Vikings had a chance to win a Super Bowl and there have been times this season where it would be hard to argue. There have been other points, however, when missed tackles and defensive mistakes appear to have the ability to derail the Vikings' success.

"I tell you what," tight end Visanthe Shiancoe said. "If we fix our mistakes, and we made a lot of mistakes today, we are a Super Bowl caliber team."

2009 Regular Season
November 8, 2009

He wears it well

Turns out Brett Favre looks great in purple. His play has exceeded all expectations and helped put the Vikings in prime position in the NFC.

Judd Zulgad, *StarTribune*

The circus act the Vikings put themselves through to get Brett Favre was worth it.

Sure, it might have caused a few headaches, but eight games into the season, there is little doubt coach Brad Childress and owner Zygi Wilf would do it all again.

The Vikings are enjoying their bye week with a 7-1 record and a 2 1/2-game lead in the NFC North. Along with New Orleans (7-0), they appear to be the class of the conference, and the 40-year-old quarterback with the surgically repaired biceps tendon and the partially torn rotator cuff, not to mention an assortment of other aches and pains, is a major reason.

His 16 touchdown passes tie him for the NFL lead, and his 106.0 passer rating is fourth-best. Plus, he has thrown only three interceptions.

"He's a coach and a player at the same time," said Sidney Rice, who has emerged as the Vikings' leading receiver in large part because of Favre. "He's been in this game 19 seasons, he knows what's going on out there at all times. He's just talking to us, staying in the receivers' ears, letting us know what he's thinking, and he'll tell us out there on the field. Right there in the huddle and we'll just run with it."

Favre, who received a two-year, $25 million contract that included $12 million in guarantees, has brought more than anyone could have expected.

Criticized by some Jets teammates last season for an aloof demeanor, Favre has blended in with his new teammates. He has two lockers at Winter Park (so does running back Adrian Peterson) but makes no obvious attempt to avoid anyone.

An early report that Favre's late decision to join the Vikings caused a "schism" has resulted in a running joke among players who now frequently use a word that several had never heard previously.

But all the goodwill Favre has off the field wouldn't mean anything if he wasn't producing on it.

So far, so good

Many thought Favre would serve as the game manager of a West Coast system he ran for 16 seasons in Green Bay. That theory was bolstered in a season-opening victory at Cleveland as Favre completed 14 of 21 passes for 110 yards in a 34-20 victory. Peterson was the star that day, rushing for 180 yards and three touchdowns.

But as opposing defenses made it obvious they were going to focus on stopping the run, the Vikings altered their approach. Before Favre's arrival, even if a team keyed on Peterson, he was still the best option. Favre has changed that and subsequently created nightmares for defensive coordinators.

After attempting 48 passes in the first two weeks, Favre came within two of that total in Week 3 against the 49ers. His final throw, a 32-yarder on which Greg Lewis made a remarkable catch in the back of the end zone, pulled out a 27-24 victory. Favre also engineered a fourth-quarter comeback in a 33-31 victory over Baltimore in Week 6 after the Vikings defense had a late meltdown.

Then there are the two victories over the Packers in which Favre threw for seven touchdowns with no interceptions. The latest came last week at Lambeau Field as Favre, booed throughout, threw a season-high four touchdown passes to four receivers.

Asked what Favre has meant to the Vikings,

Peterson quickly responded: "The world. You guys are seeing it firsthand. The things that he's doing on the field and along with a lot of guys. ... Offensively, we have so many weapons and so many ways to threaten people. I'm loving it. With Brett back there at quarterback and all the talent we have surrounding him, the sky's the limit."

However, eight regular-season games still remain, and a potential playoff run. And it gets a bit dicey in trying to determine whether Favre can continue at this high level.

Dome sweet domes

Last season, Favre completed 70.6 percent of his passes in the Jets' first 11 games and had 20 touchdowns and 13 interceptions. In the final five games, four of them losses, he threw for only two touchdowns and had nine interceptions. In fairness to Favre, he was battling a biceps injury and did not have the offensive weapons the 2009 Vikings possess.

But the reality is that Favre's play before and after his 12th game of the regular season hasn't been the same the past four years. During the Packers' 13-3 run in 2007, he had a .685 completion percentage with 22 touchdowns and eight interceptions in the first 11 games and a .591 completion percentage with six touchdowns and seven interceptions in the last five.

The Vikings are limiting Favre's throws in practice as a precaution, and for the first time in his career, he gets to play his home games indoors during the cold-weather months.

The Vikings will close out November with three consecutive home games. Their only cold-weather contest will be at Chicago on Monday night, Dec. 28. Three of their five December games likely will be indoors -- Arizona has a retractable roof -- and the Dec. 20 night game in Carolina might be chilly but probably not frigid.

As Favre stood in a cramped interview room at Lambeau last Sunday, he acknowledged that plenty of things must play out before any judgment is made about this season.

"We'll find out how good we are," he said. "We've had some tough tests. For the most part, we've responded very well. As I've said when talking about this football team, how good this team could be, it also has not done anything yet, other than be 7-1. Granted, that's pretty good. At this point, we've put ourselves in a good position. There are things we can get better at. ... But it's a pretty good position to be in at the bye week."

2009 Regular Season
November 12, 2009

Favre stands to benefit from Vikings' bye-week break

The quarterback used the time off to go hunting, but the extra rest figures to help him recover from nagging injuries to his ankle, knee, foot and groin.

Judd Zulgad, *StarTribune*

For the first time since he signed with the Vikings in late August, Brett Favre was able to get away from football last week. The quarterback remained in town during the team's bye week -- he did spend part of a day watching film at Winter Park -- but Favre also was able to enjoy some time in the woods, hunting.

So what did he kill? "Time," Favre said Wednesday during his midweek news conference.

Favre wasn't complaining. The Vikings' break might have stifled a bit of the momentum for a team that will take a 7-1 record into Sunday's game against Detroit, but the 40-year-old Favre stands to benefit from the rest.

During the first half of the season, Favre dealt with ankle, knee, foot and hip issues. Actually, according to him, the hip problem is really a groin injury he suffered in practice the Wednesday before he threw a season-high four touchdown passes in a 38-26 victory on Nov. 1 in his return to Lambeau Field.

Favre has played through an assortment of injuries throughout his 19-year career -- Sunday will mark his 300th consecutive game, including playoffs -- but said this is the first time he has dealt with a groin strain.

"I think I'll be fine," said Favre, who was limited in practice Wednesday because of what is now listed as a hip/groin injury by the Vikings. "That's something that, for me, I've always said you have to have muscles to pull them. Either that's a sign of old age or I'm developing muscles for the first time in my career.

"It was a concern for the [Packers] game. I made it through. With a week's rest I think I'll be fine, but I'm not going to make a bigger issue than it is. It's kind of a new thing for me. Play 18-some-odd years and not have anything like that. That probably worried me more than anything."

While Favre did not seem concerned Wednesday, the Vikings can't be blamed for being extra-cautious with him. He struggled late last season with the New York Jets because of a partially torn biceps tendon, and there were many skeptics who were convinced that at his age he would struggle to get through this season without any setbacks.

But Favre said mentally and physically he feels "pretty good" halfway through his first season in Minnesota. His statistics reflect that, as he's ranked second in the NFL with a 106.0 passer rating. New Orleans' Drew Brees (106.1) is first. Favre also has 16 touchdown passes and only three interceptions, putting him among the league leaders on the good side in both those categories.

"It's hard for me to say what I thought I would feel like, but I know that if you had asked, 'What would our record be at this point?' Seven-and-one I think is definitely very acceptable," Favre said. "It seems like the better you do, the expectations even get higher. I'm very pleased with where we are but the expectations will continue to get higher. Not only from internally but from everyone else. I consider that a good thing but we have a lot of football left.

"Physically I've handled it ... I don't want to say better than I expected because I came in expecting to play every game. And when I addressed it at the start of the season saying, 'I have no idea what to expect.' I don't. But it's been a lot of fun. It's everything I thought it would be."

Favre and the Vikings' success figures to

continue against the woeful Lions (1-7), a team that he has gone 24-9 against during the regular season in his career. That's his most victories against any opponent.

Favre threw for two touchdowns and 155 yards in the Vikings' 27-13 victory over Detroit at Ford Field in Week 2. He has not thrown for fewer than 232 yards in a game since then.

Favre's improvement in the Vikings' system hasn't been lost on Lions coach Jim Schwartz. "When we played them earlier in the season he was a little bit more game-managing," Schwartz said. "They were running the ball effectively like they do and they weren't leaning a whole lot on Brett Favre. "But as it's going, in every game, they've added a little bit more, and they've done a little bit more, put a little more on his shoulders, and he has put the team on his shoulders a couple of times."

That included against the Packers in Lambeau only days after Favre hurt his groin.

"I'd like to say it [happened] in a full-tackling drill but it was a lot less than that," Favre said of how he got hurt. "It was really just a half-walkthrough rolling out to the right. It's like when you wake up in the morning and you're putting your shoes on and your back gives out for no apparent reason."

The Vikings can only hope this injury was simply a one-time deal for Favre and not the beginning of any type of trend.

2009 Regular Season — Vikings 27/Detroit 10 — November 16, 2009

When Favre flings a pass, it's 'Showtime' for a young receiver

Jim Souhan, StarTribune

Along with "They are who we thought they were" and "We never talk about what we talk about," Dennis Green's greatest contribution to football lexicon may have been his description of Cris Carter's elastic capabilities as a receiver.

Green like to say that Carter "expanded the field," meaning his ability to catch balls thrown out of bounds while keeping his feet in play, to leap and dive for errant passes, increased his target size exponentially. Most receivers, to a quarterback under pressure, resemble a dart board; Carter looked more like a Ferris wheel.

Current Vikings receivers coach George Stewart calls that useable arc a receiver's "catch radius." Sidney Rice's seems to be expanding like a party balloon attached to an air compressor.

Sunday afternoon at the Metrodome, Brett Favre threw passes toward Rice casually as a beachcomber might toss shells into the surf. Rice caught seven of the eight Favre threw his way, gaining 201 yards, the fourth-highest total in Vikings history, in a 27-10 victory over Detroit.

He dropped a late pass from Tarvaris Jackson that might have given Rice the team record now held by Sammy White, who had a 210-yard game in 1976. As Favre's confidence in Rice's reactions and radius increases, he may get another chance to break that record before the season ends.

"I talk about the relationship with he and Brett," Vikings coach Brad Childress said. "Brett says to me on the sideline, 'They just can't stop him.' I said to Brett, 'You have the same agent, or what?'"

Most athletic relationships are born of success or necessity. Favre and Rice have little in common. Sunday, Favre played his 36th career game against the Lions; Rice has played 35 total games in the NFL. They've played nine games together now, and in those nine games Favre has helped transform Rice from a part-time possession receiver to the best receiver on one of football's best teams. Rice has caught 44 passes for 786 yards and a 17.9 yards per catch, easily giving Rice the team lead in each category.

"Sidney has a great catch radius, and that's one thing we saw out of him when he was coming out of South Carolina," Stewart said. "He can catch the football as well as anyone in this league. He might not be the fastest guy in the world, but he understands football, and he gets the most out of his ability."

Favre told Vikings staffers that he noticed a catch Rice made against the Packers in 2007 and thought Rice had star potential. Adrian Peterson foretold a big season for Rice, giving him the nickname "Showtime" this summer.

"I told Sidney, 'This will be a luxury for me, to be able to throw the ball up and for you to bail me out,'" Favre said. "He's done that numerous times."

As spectacularly as Favre has played this season, he no longer displays his signature arm strength on long passes. Twice on Sunday Favre threw a long lob in Rice's general direction, and both times Rice swerved from his defender to make a diving catch, once appearing to push away from the defensive back with a force that would have made Carter proud.

"Speed obviously helps with separation, but sometimes a guy's worst enemy is his speed," Favre said.

Favre compared Rice's body control to that of

a rebounder in basketball, for whom fighting for position and timing his jump are as important as size and innate athletic ability.

"A ball is up in front of 70,000, that's 50 yards downfield, that's just hanging up there, and you've got guys draped on you, that has to be pretty tough to adjust to," Favre said. "He makes it look pretty easy."

Rice worked out this summer with Cardinals star Larry Fitzgerald and Carter. Now that he has a star's nickname and statistics, might we see Rice develop the egomania often associated with the position?

Probably not. Rice calls interviewers "Sir," speaks quietly, and when he dropped that last pass on Sunday, he did 25 pushups on the sideline as penance. "He's an outstanding kid," Stewart said. "You need to get to know him."

A nation's football fans might do just that, and soon.

2009 Regular Season — Vikings 27/Detroit 10 — November 16, 2009

Unclean sweep letdowns are troubling, but not the final outcome

Judd Zulgad, StarTribune

Any question about just how big the differences are between the NFC North champion Vikings from 2008 and the 2009 edition destined to repeat as division champs might have been answered in the team's games against Detroit the past two years.

Last season, the Vikings swept the woeful (and eventually winless) Lions by an unimpressive total of six points. This season, the Vikings swept the still-feeble Lions (1-8) by the combined margin of 31 points.

And in neither game did the Vikings play their best. That included a 27-10 victory Sunday before an announced crowd of 63,854 at the Metrodome that left the Vikings (8-1) behind only New Orleans (9-0) for supremacy in the NFC. It also gave the Vikings a 4-0 record against division opponents as they began the second half of their season.

"It feels good to be 8-1, but we're trying to be 15-1," Vikings tight end Visanthe Shiancoe said. "We're taking it one step at a time, one brick at a time to build this building, because we are building an empire here."

That talk is a bit premature, but the Vikings certainly have an offense that ranks among the NFL's best. Three years after coach Brad Childress caused guffaws throughout the Twin Cities by claiming the West Coast offense could kick the behind of opponents when executed properly, Childress is now frequently getting the last laugh.

Sunday's offensive highlights included Adrian Peterson's 133 rushing yards on 18 carries and two touchdowns; Brett Favre's season-high 344 yards passing and one touchdown with no interceptions; and Sidney Rice's 201 receiving yards, a figure that left him 9 shy of Sammy White's franchise single-game record set in 1976.

The Vikings had five plays of 40 or more yards. Among the highlights were a pair of 43-yard passes by Favre to Rice in the second quarter and a 56-yarder in the fourth that set up the Vikings' final touchdown. Rookie wide receiver Percy Harvin turned a short fourth-quarter gain into a long reception when he bounced off linebacker DeAndre Levy and proceeded to dash 40 yards.

Peterson contributed a 22-yard touchdown run in the second quarter, and appeared destined to be headed toward a 61-yard score later in the quarter when Lions cornerback Phillip Buchanon caught him and punched the ball out from behind at the Lions 18. Detroit recovered the ball in the end zone. That was the second lost fumble charged to Peterson; the first came when Harvin was unable to hang on to a pitch from the running back on a reverse in the first quarter.

"We didn't do a great job of holding on to the football," Childress said. "I thought we did a great job of moving the football up and down the field, but the ball has to come with you. That is incumbent on what you are doing. We had a chance to put some distance in there and not be sweating as you go to the locker room. It's not for lack of trying."

Said Favre: "I know there are a lot of things we've got to correct. Obviously we only got 10 points on 300 yards [in the first half]. However, you look at it I think we can score more points."

Areas of concern for Childress will include a 3-for-11 conversion rate on third down -- the Vikings were only 6-for-22 on third down against the Lions this season -- and a season-high 13 penalties for 91 yards. The Vikings entered the game as fifth-least-penalized team in the NFL and had been called for only three infractions in a 38-

2009 Regular Season — Vikings 27/Detroit 10
November 16, 2009

26 victory at Green Bay in their final game before the bye.

"The penalty thing is disturbing to me," Childress said.

Given the Vikings' success, and Detroit's lack of it, it wouldn't have been a stretch to believe that Childress' players wouldn't have been at their most focused on Sunday. Although having only a seven-point cushion in the third quarter seemed to be an indication that was the case, Childress didn't see it as an issue.

"I thought our guys were loose, but I learned a long time ago they don't have to be sitting there rocking in the chair to play good football," he said. "They were loose, they were fresh. The question is, would you say we were too loose? We were too loose with the football, I know that. But certainly played decently on the defensive side. There are just some things we have to tighten up. Improving is the key. You want to continue to ascend."

The Vikings will resume working on that goal Wednesday after getting today off. Rice, for one, is looking forward to the opportunity to continue making a productive offense that much better.

"We're doing a decent job, but we have lots of room for improvement," Rice said. "There's a lot of things we can still work on. Had a couple of missed assignments out there today, and hopefully we're going to continue to fight to try to get to that level to get to the team that we want to be."

2009 Photo Gallery

Purple Reign! GALLERY

GALLERY

Purple Reign!

GALLERY

PURPLE REIGN! GALLERY

GALLERY

GALLERY

Purple Reign!

GALLERY

GALLERY

Purple Reign!

GALLERY

Purple Reign!

GALLERY

PURPLE REIGN! GALLERY

GALLERY

WHAT's NEXT?